Cambridge Certificate of Proficiency in English 5

WITH ANSWERS

*Examination papers from
University of Cambridge
ESOL Examinations:
English for Speakers of
Other Languages*

CAMBRIDGE
UNIVERSITY PRESS

CAMBRIDGE UNIVERSITY PRESS
Cambridge, New York, Melbourne, Madrid, Cape Town, Singapore,
São Paulo, Delhi, Dubai, Tokyo

Cambridge University Press
The Edinburgh Building, Cambridge CB2 8RU, UK

www.cambridge.org
Information on this title: www.cambridge.org/9780521672757

First published 2006
6th printing 2010

Printed in the United Kingdom at the University Press, Cambridge

A catalogue record for this publication is available from the British Library

ISBN 978-0-521-67274-0 Student's Book
ISBN 978-0-521-67275-7 Student's Book with answers
ISBN 978-0-521-67277-1 Audio Cassettes (2)
ISBN 978-0-521-67278-8 Audio CDs (2)
ISBN 978-0-521-67279-5 Self-study Pack (Student's Book with answers and Audio CDs (2))

Contents

Thanks and acknowledgements

The authors and publishers are grateful to the following for permission to use copyright material. While every effort has been made, it has not been possible to identify the sources to all of the material used and in such cases the publishers would welcome information from the copyright owners. Apologies are expressed for any omissions.

The publishers are grateful to the following for permission to reproduce copyright material:

For the extract on p. 8: adapted from 'The Tin Tin Book' by James Delingpole, *The Daily Telegraph*, 6 October 2001; for the extract on pp. 60–61: adapted from 'Shopping in Europe' by Victoria Glendinning, *The Daily Telegraph*, 9 December 2000; for the extract on pp. 66–67: adapted from 'Spontaneous Combustion' by Martin Gayford, *The Daily Telegraph*, 10 March 2001. © Telegraph Group Limited; for the extract on p. 9: adapted from 'Underground, Overground', *Geographical Magazine*, October 2000. Used by permission of Circle Publishing; for the extract on p. 9: 'Sadie and her son' adapted from *Morecambe before Wise*. Reprinted by permission of Harper Collins Publishers Ltd. © Graham McCann, 1998; for the extract on p. 10: 'The cricket tour', adapted from *Over to you Aggers*, by Jonathon Agnew; for the extract on p. 27: from *Covenant of the Wild*, by Stephen Budianksy, for the extract on p. 68: 'Sound and fury', adapted from *Over Here*, by Raymond Seitz. Used by permission of The Orion Publishing Group; for the extract on p. 11: 'Industrial relations in football' and for the extract on p. 34: 'Professional Sport' from *Staying Up*, by Rick Gekoski. Used by permission of Time Warner Book Group; for the extract on p. 12: adapted from 'Why do we need sport?' by Alyson Rudd, *The Times MM Supplement*, December 1999; for the extract on p. 13: adapted from 'Watch Out Wimbledon' by Doug Sager, *The Times Weekend*, 13 June 1998. © Times Newspapers Limited; for the extract on pp. 14–15: from 'The Play' adapted from *Atonement*. © 2001 by Ian McEwan; for the extract on p. 37: adapted from *Amsterdam*. © 1999 Ian McEwan. Published by Jonathon Cape, Doubleday and Alfred Knopf, Canada; for the extract on p. 42: 'Sam and his father' adapted from *White* by Rosie Thomas. Published by Heinemann/Arrow; for the adapted extract on p. 47: from *Sleep Solution* by Nigel Ball, published by Vermilion and Ulysses Press. Reprinted by permission of The Random House Group Ltd; for the extract on p. 26: 'Our Animals and Other Family' by Roger Scruton, *The Business FT Weekend Magazine*, 10 February 2001. Used by kind permission of Roger Scruton; for the extract on p. 35: adapted from 'Are you being served?' by Guy Diamond, *Time Out Eating and Drinking 2002*. Used by kind permission of Time Out Guides Ltd; for the extract on p. 36: adapted from 'The Sea' *Art Review*, July/August 2001. Used by permission of Art Review; for the extract on p. 38: adapted from pp.23–26 *Wild Ice, Antarctic Journeys* by Ron Naveen. © 1990. Used by kind permission of Mr Ron Naveen; for the extract on p. 39: adapted from 'Rhyme or Reason' by Paul Evans, *BBC Wildlife Magazine* March 2000; for the extract on p. 87: adapted from 'Not just a pretty Polly' by Tamsin Constable, *BBC Wildlife Magazine* March 2002; for the extract on p. 98: adapted from 'The fall of a sparrow' by Stephen Moss, *BBC Wildlife Magazine*, November 2001. Used by permission of BBC Wildlife Magazine; for the extract on pp. 40–41: adapted from 'How I baked in Alaska' by Nicholas Woodsworth,

Financial Times weekend travel, 10 February 2001, for the extract on p. 90: adapted from 'I cannot write poetically' by Michael Church, *Financial Times Weekend*, 2 September 2000; for the extract on p. 91: adapted from 'Hot Shots II' by Ludovic Hunter-Tilney, *Financial Times Weekend*, 14 July 2001. © The Financial Times Limited; for the extract on p. 46: adapted from *Microbes, Bugs and Wonder Drugs*. Reproduced with permission from F Balkwill and M Rolph. © Fran Balkwill; for the extracts on pp. 52–53: adapted from *The Family History Book* by Stella Colwell. © 1980. Used by kind permission of Stella Colwell; for the extract on p. 61: adapted from 'Smile Like a star' by Jacqui Ripley, *Now Magazine*. © Now/IPC+ Syndication; for the extract on p. 64: adapted from *Nick Drake* by Patrick Humphries. Published by Bloomsbury. Used by permission of Bloomsbury Publishing; for the extract on p. 65: adapted from 'Thinking like an Adman' by Meg Carter, *The Independent* 22 June 1995; for the extract on p. 105: adapted from 'Car-sharing is non-starter for most Britons' by Nicholas Pyke, *The Independent*, 29 April 2001. © The Independent News & Media (UK) Limited; for the extract on p. 86: adapted from *Free to Trade* by Michael Ridpath, published by Mandarin Publishing. Used by permission of Blake Friedmann Literary Agency Limited; for the extract on p. 87: adapted from *The Intelligent Organisation* by Pinchot. © 1996. Reprinted with permission Berrett-Koehler Publishers Inc, San Francisco, CA. All rights reserved. www.bkconnection.com; for the extract on p. 89: 'Frank Sinatra's Press Agent' from *His Way* by Kitty Kelly, copyright © 1986 by H B Productions Inc. Used by permission of Bantam Books, a division of Random House Inc; for the extract on pp. 92–93: adapted from 'Blind to change' by Laura Spinney, *New Scientist*, 18 November 2000. Used by permission of New Scientist; for the extract on p. 94: 'Getting a life' by Kathryn Hughes. This is an edited extract of an article that first appeared in the November 1998 issue of *Prospect Magazine* (www.prospect-magazine.co.uk); for the extract on p. 99: adapted from *The Secret Language of Dreams* by David Fontana. Copyright Duncan Baird Publishers (1994).

The publishers are grateful to the following for permission to include photographs:

For p.C2 (a) (Getty Images/AFP/Martyn Hayhow); (b) (Alamy/ImageState); (c) (Punchstock/Brand X Pictures/PNC; (d) (Rex Features/Karl Schoendorfer); for p.C3 (e) (Rex Features/Eddie Mulholland); (f) (Getty Images/Gianni Cigolini); (g) (Alamy/Hortus/Cidny Lewis); for p.C4 (Alamy/Fredrik Skold); for p.C6 (a) (Getty Images/Daniel Bosler); (b) (Rex Features/CNP); (c) (Getty Images/K-P Wolf); for p.C7 (d) (Getty Images/David Woolley); (e) (Rex Features/Sunset); (f) Getty Images/Kaluzny-Thatcher); for p.C8 (a) (Rex Features/Paul Childs); (b) (Corbis/Ralf Schultheiss/zefa); (c) (Rex Features/Peter Brooker); for p.C9 (d) Punchstock/Digital Vision); (e) (Robbie Jack Photography); (f) (Alamy/Aflo Foto Agency); (g) (Jupiter Images/Creatas).

Picture research by Suzanne Williams / Pictureresearch.co.uk

Cover design by Dunne & Scully

The recordings which accompany this book were made at Studio AVP, London.

Introduction

This collection of four complete practice tests comprises past papers from the University of Cambridge ESOL Examinations Certificate of Proficiency in English (CPE) examination; students can practise these tests on their own or with the help of a teacher.

The CPE examination is part of a group of examinations developed by Cambridge ESOL called the Cambridge Main Suite. The Main Suite consists of five examinations which have similar characteristics but are designed for different levels of English language ability. Within the five levels, CPE is at Level C2 in the *Council of Europe's Common European Framework of Reference for Languages: Learning, teaching, assessment*. It has also been accredited by the Qualifications and Curriculum Authority in the UK as a Level 3 ESOL certificate in the National Qualifications Framework. The CPE examination is recognised by the majority of British universities for English language entrance requirements, and is taken by candidates in over 100 countries throughout the world. Around 75% of the candidates are 25 years of age or under, whilst around 12% are 31 years old or over.

Examination	Council of Europe Framework Level	UK National Qualifications Framework Level
CPE Certificate of Proficiency in English	C2	3
CAE Certificate in Advanced English	C1	2
FCE First Certificate in English	B2	1
PET Preliminary English Test	B1	Entry 3
KET Key English Test	A2	Entry 2

Further information

The information contained in this practice book is designed to be an overview of the exam. For a full description of all of the above exams including information about task types, testing focus and preparation, please see the relevant handbooks which can be obtained from Cambridge ESOL at the address below or from the website at: www.CambridgeESOL.org

University of Cambridge ESOL Examinations
1 Hills Road
Cambridge CB1 2EU
United Kingdom

Telephone: +44 1223 553355
Fax: +44 1223 460278
e-mail: ESOLHelpdesk@CambridgeESOL.org

The structure of CPE: an overview

The CPE examination consists of five papers:

Paper 1   Reading 1 hour 30 minutes
This paper consists of four parts with 40 questions, which take the form of three multiple-choice tasks and a gapped text task. Part 1 contains three short texts, Part 2 contains four short texts and Parts 3 and 4 each contain one longer text. The texts are taken from fiction, non-fiction, journals, magazines, newspapers, and promotional and informational materials. This paper is designed to test candidates' ability to understand the meaning of written English at word, phrase, sentence, paragraph and whole text level.

Paper 2   Writing 2 hours
This paper consists of two writing tasks in a range of formats (e.g. letter, report, review, article, essay, proposal). Candidates are asked to complete two tasks, writing between 300 and 350 words for each. Part 1 (Question 1) consists of one compulsory task based on instructions and a short text or texts. Part 2 (Questions 2–5) consists of one task which candidates select from a choice of four. Question 5 has a task on each of the three set texts. Candidates choose one of the tasks in Question 5, if they want to answer on a set text. Assessment is based on achievement of task, range and accuracy of vocabulary and grammatical structures, organisation and appropriacy of register and format.

Paper 3   Use of English 1 hour 30 minutes
This paper consists of five parts with 44 questions. These take the form of an open cloze, a word formation task, gapped sentences, key word transformations and two texts with comprehension questions and a summary writing task. The two texts are from different sources and represent different treatments of the same topic. This paper is designed to assess candidates' ability to demonstrate knowledge and control of the English language system by setting tasks at both whole text and sentence level.

Paper 4   Listening 40 minutes (approximately)
This paper consists of four parts with 28 questions, which take the form of two multiple-choice tasks, a sentence-completion task and a three-way matching task. Part 1 contains four short extracts and Parts 2 to 4 each contain one longer text. The texts are audio-recordings based on a variety of sources including interviews, discussions, lectures, conversations and documentary features. The paper is designed to assess candidates' ability to understand the meaning of spoken English, to extract information from a spoken text and to understand speakers' attitudes and opinions.

Paper 5   Speaking 19 minutes
The Speaking test consists of three parts, which take the form of an interview section, a collaborative task and individual long turns with follow-up discussion. The standard test format is two candidates and two examiners.

Grading

The overall CPE grade is based on the total score gained in all five papers. It is not necessary to achieve a satisfactory level in all five papers in order to pass the examination. Certificates are given to candidates who pass the examination with grade A, B or C. A is the highest. The minimum successful performance in order to achieve a grade C corresponds to about 60% of the total marks. D and E are failing grades. Every candidate receives a Statement of Results which includes a graphical profile of their performance in each paper and shows their relative performance in each one. Each paper is weighted to 40 marks. Therefore, the five CPE papers total 200 marks, after weighting.

For further information on grading and results, go to the website (see page 5).

Test 1

PAPER 1   READING (1 hour 30 minutes)

Part 1

For questions **1–18**, read the three texts below and decide which answer (**A**, **B**, **C** or **D**) best fits each gap.

Mark your answers **on the separate answer sheet**.

The Tintin books

What is so special about Georges 'Hergé' Rémi's tales of the adventures of a boy called Tintin, created for a newspaper in Belgium in the 1920s, that they should have **(1)** .... being translated into more than 50 languages and selling more than 120 million copies? How is it that they have managed to endure for so long? One reason may be Hergé's extraordinary attention to detail. He constantly revised and improved Tintin's original black-and-white adventures to make them more **(2)** .... to new audiences. And he based all his illustrations on an extensive personal library of photographs which he **(3)** .... over the years.

In a career of more than 50 years, Hergé produced only 24 Tintin books. Had he been less meticulous, he might well have been a lot more **(4)** .... , but I doubt he would have been so widely loved and admired. Picking up a Tintin book the other day for the first time in many years, I found myself **(5)** .... between the urge to race through the story and an **(6)** .... to linger on the visual detail.

1	**A** turned out	**B** finished off	**C** come to	**D** ended up
2	**A** relevant	**B** apt	**C** applicable	**D** fitting
3	**A** amassed	**B** mustered	**C** convened	**D** swelled
4	**A** abundant	**B** prolific	**C** fruitful	**D** profuse
5	**A** pulled	**B** drawn	**C** lured	**D** torn
6	**A** impetus	**B** incentive	**C** impulse	**D** intuition

Cave fauna

For the past 35 years a professor of zoology named Valerio Sbordoni has explored the caves and underground chambers of Mexico in search of new forms of life. He has found these in abundance, to say the least. To **(7)** …. Sbordoni has discovered more than 150 species of **(8)** …. unknown cave-dwelling creatures. In one chamber **(9)** …. , he found over forty **(10)** …. species of butterfly, an incredible variety for such an inhospitable environment.

Many of these species, Sbordoni believes, **(11)** …. underground millions of years ago to avoid extinction and adapted to life beneath the earth's surface. Obviously, conditions for life underground are far from ideal, and Sbordoni believes that only severe climatic changes, probably caused by shifting glaciers, could **(12)** …. such a migration.

7 **A** now	**B** present	**C** today	**D** date
8 **A** hitherto	**B** hereby	**C** henceforth	**D** herewith
9 **A** exclusively	**B** only	**C** alone	**D** solely
10 **A** dissimilar	**B** distinct	**C** disparate	**D** disconnected
11 **A** retired	**B** shrank	**C** retreated	**D** departed
12 **A** conjure up	**B** account for	**C** bear out	**D** carry off

Sadie and her son

A combination of boredom and, increasingly, absenteeism, ensured that the standard of Eric's work declined alarmingly. Sadie, who had hoped that her son would do well at school, was too **(13)** …. a mother to have remained unaware of the problem for very long, but when the school reports started to **(14)** …. just how poorly he was faring, she felt shocked and angry.

One report **(15)** …. curtly that Eric was 45th out of 49 pupils. Sadie, typically, was determined that her son should arrest his dizzying decline as speedily as possible and then – she hoped – start to improve. She visited the school and offered to pay for further tuition but was told, 'It would be money down the **(16)** …. .' This rejection only seemed to **(17)** …. Sadie on in her search for a suitable career for Eric. It surprised no one who knew her that she reacted to the undeniably **(18)** …. disappointment of this setback in such a remarkably spirited and positive manner.

13 **A** engrossed	**B** mindful	**C** riveted	**D** attentive
14 **A** proclaim	**B** advocate	**C** denote	**D** underline
15 **A** professed	**B** announced	**C** aired	**D** uttered
16 **A** pipe	**B** drain	**C** sink	**D** gutter
17 **A** spur	**B** press	**C** incite	**D** boost
18 **A** vivid	**B** stark	**C** bitter	**D** hard

Part 2

You are going to read four extracts which are all concerned in some way with sport. For questions **19–26**, choose the answer (**A, B, C** or **D**) which you think fits best according to the text.

Mark your answers **on the separate answer sheet**.

The Cricket Tour

As the plane took off for the England cricket tour to Australia, I was facing a challenge. Less than six weeks earlier I had been a professional cricketer, but since then I had switched camps and joined the press corps. While many other cricketers have retired to write about the game, none had started their new careers at the sharp end in the world of tabloid journalism. I was only too aware of the manner in which the majority of players viewed the press. 'Vultures,' was what I had heard one call them a few years before, and I wondered how long it would be before I, too, was dismissed in that derogatory fashion.

To make matters worse, I knew that my presence had provoked a feeling of resentment in more than one of the journalists on that plane. It was not a personal dislike but concern, based on self-preservation, that a cricketer with little or no training could just saunter in and take an experienced reporter's job. So I was most relieved to find that I was sitting next to Colin Bateman of the *Daily Express*, whom I had known for some time. We had become friends. Now, however, we would be in direct competition. I asked him if he was planning to write anything that night.

'Of course,' he retorted.

'But all we've done is got on a plane.'

With a wry smile he replied: 'Welcome to journalism.'

19 What made the writer different from other retired cricketers who had become writers?

    A how recent his experience of being a player was

    B the kind of newspaper he had gone to work for

    C his acceptance of the fact that players would now dislike him

    D the nature of his relationships with other cricketers

20 What does the writer imply about some of the other journalists on the plane?

    A They realised that he would have an advantage over them.

    B They instinctively regarded newcomers to their group with suspicion.

    C Their attitude resulted from lack of confidence in their own abilities.

    D Their disapproval of his presence was understandable.

Industrial relations in football

Industrial relations in football in Britain, it seems, are tied to a form of language that makes measured assessment difficult and causes ill feeling by its very nature. Just as player–manager relations are conducted in the outdated language of the traditional factory floor, so the terminology used to describe changing jobs, 'buying' and 'selling' players, distorts the reality. Both sides suffer from this: the management accuses some players of greed or disloyalty, while the players feel the club treats them cynically, as if they were disposable objects.

In the real world, though, people move from one job to another all the **line 9** time. They aren't bought or sold, they resign, sign a new contract with another business, have a change. Sometimes, if they have signed a long-term contract, their old employers refuse to let them go, or demand to be compensated. In fact, life in the corporate world is generally less well paid, less secure and more demanding than it is in the world of professional football. The resentment that players feel about 'being sold' is probably created more by the language used to describe the process than by the process itself. This all has a tendency to descend into stereotypes: the gentleman chairman who considers himself a model of good business behaviour, and the hypersensitive player who thinks he is being treated as a disposable commodity.

21 What is the writer's point about employment in 'the real world' (line 9)?

    A It involves using terminology that avoids the reality of situations.

    B It has similarities with employment in the world of football.

    C It is something that football players would not be suited to.

    D It operates on a more logical basis than employment in football.

22 What does the writer imply about football players in the extract as a whole?

    A They have no genuine cause for complaint about the way they are treated.

    B They have too high an opinion of their own worth.

    C They pretend that they are not primarily motivated by selfish aims.

    D They are the victims of an outdated system.

Why do we need sport?

Spectators play vicariously when watching football. After ninety minutes of a close match between your team and the local rivals, you can feel palpable exhaustion. Just as when you are in a car being driven at speed by someone you do not trust, during the match you kick every ball and feel the agony of every shot that goes off-target. The tribalism of sport is well documented. It is just play – dressing in the team colours, crying when you lose in the final – but it enriches lives. The players themselves kiss, stamp, shout and perform cartwheels, but they are being paid to play and have to perform in front of hundreds or thousands or even millions of critical supporters.

We all need sport to exert our freedom of spirit in this polite and ordered world. We need to be able to cavort and weep, to swear and sweat, to want to win at all costs when the cost is nothing. In sport we experience pure joy, there is no sense of our place in any hierarchy, and we feel warm when we remember our most recent triumph.

23 Which of the following does the writer imply with regard to football spectators?

    A   They lack control over events.

    B   They have unrealistic expectations.

    C   They are ashamed of their behaviour.

    D   They have a sense of superiority.

24 In the second paragraph, the writer says that sport is important because it

    A   enables people to confront their fears.

    B   improves people's self-esteem.

    C   brings people together in a common cause.

    D   takes people's minds off serious matters.

The Tennis Coach

The verdict was: 'You can be fixed.' My long-time tennis guru volleyed the ball across the net with a grin which seemed to threaten as much as it promised. My elbow ached and my feet pinched in this season's shoes. But I believed. Therefore I was here, on the courts of the Hotel Hermitage – like an old banger rolled into the body shop, ready and willing to be fixed.

I was a vintage model – slow to start, running erratically – and my game was riddled with rust spots. It took a master craftsman like Mark Nickless to pound out the dents in my forehand and put some spring back into my suspension. This latter fix was accomplished in seconds. He showed me how to hit from the legs, instead of windmilling my arms. The ache in my elbow ceased.

My mechanic was a Californian whom I have followed around the world as he perfected his idiosyncratic teaching technique in a dozen resorts. 'Location, location, location,' he intoned, drawing lines in the clay to show that for each shot I delivered across the net there was only one perfect position. Being in the right place not only reduces the wear and tear of racing mindlessly around the court, it allowed me to focus on the way the point was likely to develop. 'Anticipation,' Nickless said, 'wins more points than perspiration.'

Not that there was not a lot of sweat and swearing in the lessons ahead. But there were sublime moments, too – and breakthroughs in stroke mechanics which I prayed would stay with me, at least through the summer.

25   Which of the following does the writer emphasise during the extract?

   A   how strange he found the coach's methods
   B   how hard it was for him to improve as a player
   C   how much he trusted the coach
   D   how nervous he was during lessons

26   The writer implies that during the lessons

   A   he played shots that he will not always be able to play.
   B   he began to overestimate his abilities as a player.
   C   he made a special effort to remain calm.
   D   he could not always put in the effort required of him.

Part 3

You are going to read an extract from a novel. Seven paragraphs have been removed from the extract. Choose from the paragraphs **A–H** the one which fits each gap (**27–33**). There is one extra paragraph which you do not need to use.

Mark your answers **on the separate answer sheet**.

The Play

Briony Tallis was one of those children possessed by a desire to have the world just so. Whereas her big sister's room was a stew of unclosed books, unfolded clothes and unmade bed, Briony's was a shrine to her controlling demon: the model farm spread across a deep window ledge consisted of the usual animals, but all facing one way – towards their owner – as if about to break into song, and even the farmyard hens were neatly corralled. In fact, Briony's was the only tidy upstairs room in the house.

27

Another was a passion for secrets: in a prized varnished cabinet, a secret drawer was opened by pushing against the grain of a cleverly turned dovetail joint, and here she kept a locked diary, and a notebook written in a code of her own invention. An old tin box hidden under a removable floorboard beneath her bed contained treasures that dated back four years to her ninth birthday. But all this could not conceal from Briony the simple truth: she had no secrets.

28

The unfortunate truth was that nothing in her life was sufficiently interesting or shameful to merit hiding. None of this was particularly an affliction; or rather, it appeared so only in retrospect, once a solution had been found. At the age of eleven she wrote her first story – a foolish affair, imitative of half a dozen folk tales and lacking, she realised later, that vital knowingness about the ways of the world that compels a reader's respect.

29

Even writing out the *she saids,* the *and thens,* made her wince, and she felt foolish, appearing to know

about the emotions of an imaginary being. Self-exposure was inevitable the moment she described a character's weakness; the reader was bound to speculate that she was describing herself.

30

Her efforts received encouragement. In fact, the Tallises soon realised that the baby of the family possessed a strange mind and a facility with words. The long afternoons she spent browsing through dictionary and thesaurus made for constructions that were inept, but hauntingly so. Briony was encouraged to read her stories aloud in the library and it surprised her parents and older sister to hear their quiet girl perform so boldly, unapologetically demanding her family's total attention as she cast her narrative spell. Even without their praise and obvious pleasure, Briony could not have been held back from her writing.

31

If this was supposed to be a joke, Briony ignored it. She was on course now, and had found satisfaction on other levels; writing stories not only involved secrecy, it also gave her all the pleasures of miniaturisation.

32

Her passion for tidiness was also satisfied, for the unruly aspects of our existence could be made just so. A crisis in a heroine's life could be made to coincide with hailstones and thunder, whereas nuptials were generally blessed with good light and soft breezes. A love of order also shaped the principles of justice, with death and marriage the main engines of house-keeping, the former being set aside exclusively for the morally dubious, the latter a reward withheld until the final page.

The Trials of Arabella, the play Briony wrote for her brother's homecoming, was her first excursion into drama. She had found the transition quite effortless. It was a relief not to be writing out the *she saids,* or describing the weather or the onset of spring or her heroine's face – beauty, she had discovered, occupied a narrow band.

33	

The play may have been a melodrama, but its author had yet to hear the term. The innocent intensity with which Briony set about the project made her particularly vulnerable to failure. She could easily have welcomed her brother with another of her stories, but it was the news that her cousins were coming to stay that had prompted this leap into a new form.

A An entire world could be created in five pages, and one that was more pleasing than a model farm. The childhood of a spoiled prince could be framed within half a page, a moonlit dash through sleepy villages was one rhythmically emphatic sentence, falling in love could be achieved in a single word – a *glance*. The pages of a recently finished story seemed to vibrate in her hand with all the life they contained.

B A room near Briony's had been dusted down, new curtains had been hung and furniture carried in from other rooms. Normally, she would have been involved in these preparations, but they coincided with her two-day writing bout.

C Only when a story was finished, all fates resolved and the whole matter sealed off at both ends so it resembled, at least in this one respect, every other finished story in the world, could she feel immune, and ready to bind the chapters with string, paint or draw the cover, and take the finished work to show to her mother or her father.

D In any case, she was discovering, as had many writers before her, that not all recognition is helpful. Cecilia's enthusiasm, for example, seemed a little overstated, tainted with condescension perhaps, and intrusive too; her big sister wanted each bound story catalogued and placed on the library shelves, between Rabindranath Tagore and Quintus Tertullian.

E What was unpleasant and distasteful, on the other hand, had infinite variation. A universe reduced to what was said in it was tidiness indeed, almost to the point of nullity, and to compensate, every utterance was delivered at the extremity of some feeling or other, in the service of which the exclamation mark was indispensable.

F But this early attempt showed her that the imagination itself was a source of secrets: while she was writing a story, no one could be told. Pretending in words was too tentative, too vulnerable, too embarrassing to let anyone know.

G Her straight-backed dolls in their many-roomed mansion appeared to be under strict instructions not to touch the walls; the various thumb-sized figures to be found standing about her dressing table suggested by their even ranks and spacing a citizen's army awaiting orders. This taste for the miniature was just one aspect of an orderly spirit.

H Her wish for a harmonious, organised world denied her the reckless possibilities of wrongdoing. Mayhem and destruction were too chaotic for her tastes, and she did not have it in her to be cruel. Her effective status as an only child, as well as the relative isolation of the Tallis house, kept her, at least during the long summer holidays, from girlish intrigues with friends.

Part 4

You are going to read an extract from a book about music. For questions **34–40**, choose the answer (**A**, **B**, **C** or **D**) which you think fits best according to the text.

Mark your answers **on the separate answer sheet**.

Folk Music & Blues Music

The most crucial, as well as the most frequently over-looked, point about 'folk music' is that the constituency whom it most truly represents doesn't consider it to be 'folk music', but simply their music. 'Folk music' is, invariably, a term applied from outside the cultures and communities to which it refers. In terms of theory, 'folk music' – the traditional set of forms, styles and songs indigenous to a people, a culture or a locale – is radically distinguishable from 'art' music, of both the classical and avant-garde varieties, and from 'popular' music, mass-produced for and mass-marketed to a mass audience. In practice, it's getting harder and harder to tell them apart.

Before the advent of recording, distinctions between categories of music were not so much based on the music itself as on who it was by and for. Such distinctions were a reflection of the class system, which is not surprising since these are essentially European definitions, and reflect prevailing European social structures. European classical music operates according to a strict hierarchical structure, with the composer (the monarch, so to speak) at the top. The composer's wishes are interpreted and enforced by the conductor (the general) and carried out by the orchestra (the troops). During their lifetimes, the great composers often also functioned as the featured soloists, but after their deaths their music became fixed and formalised; those who succeeded them rarely inherited their licence to improvise.

The classic model of 'folk' is the similarly formal tradition of the Anglo-American ballads, with their fixed musical structures and set narrative lines. To perform one of these ballads, a singer is by definition required to preserve intact both its storyline and its musical setting. The Anglo-American use of the term 'folk' music implies that such music exists, simply and solely, to fulfil the needs of a particular community. They develop it by and for themselves over a period of centuries as part of a single collective process, only slightly more personal to any given individual than the shaping of a rock by water. Through oral transmission, it filters down through the generations, serving both as a touchstone of the community's history and values, and as an index of how its communal life has changed. It is this latter attribute which many traditionalists find alarming or repugnant. For them, the key element is the preservation of a piece's pure and unsullied essence, and the imposition of an alien style onto a traditional piece is deemed an act of presumption verging on outright heresy: at the very least, it effectively amputates the piece from its native roots.

In the blues world, the picture is far more complex. Blues obeys a different set of imperatives and simultaneously holds the following truths to be self-evident: yes, there is a strong and very clearly defined tradition, and, yes, its practitioners are expected to improvise freely within it, recreating it anew to meet the immediate needs of both performer and audience. There are set themes, and there are specified functions: dance songs, work songs, celebrations, laments, love songs, hate songs, and so forth. The tradition is unfixed; indeed, it demands to be freshly reinvented with each performance, recreated anew to reflect the changing needs and circumstances of its time and place. Blues artists both ancient and modern have worked from a 'common stock' of folk materials: instrumental motifs and vocal tics, melodies, lyrical tags, chord progressions and even complete songs are derived directly from the tradition, and some of them long predate the era of recording, let alone the conventional mechanics of publishing and copyright laws. What counts above all in the blues is individuality: the development of a unique and unmistakable voice, the ability to place an ineradicable personal stamp on those 'common stock' materials freely available to all. While instrumental dexterity, vocal facility and stylistic versatility are heartily respected within the blues community, what distinguishes the truly great from the merely professional is the fully realized man (or woman)'s communicated essence of self; the ability to serve as a conduit for the full gamut of human emotion, to feel those emotions with sufficient depth and intensity that those listeners might not even have known that they had. Without exception, every blues singer who has managed to pull ahead of the pack or haul himself (or herself) from the hordes of hopefuls chasing the blues-lovers' dollar has this quality. Any competent blues artist should have the ability to entertain – those who don't should simply find another line of work before they starve to death – but the measure of true mastery, from the 1920s pioneers to the contemporary brand leaders, is the scale on which performers are capable of being themselves in public. And, by extension, the depth and complexity of that self. To serve as a neutral transmitter simply doesn't cut it here.

34 What point does the writer make about the term 'folk music' in the first paragraph?

    A It is no longer possible to be clear about what it covers.

    B It has become totally outdated.

    C It is resented by certain people.

    D It is sometimes wrongly applied to certain types of music.

35 Which of the following does the writer say about European classical music?

    A Criticism of its rigid structure is commonplace.

    B Too much respect is paid to composers while they are alive.

    C It could not function without the obedience of those involved.

    D The system by which it operates affects its quality.

36 The writer uses the image of a rock to illustrate

    A the role that 'folk' music plays in people's lives.

    B the strength of the tradition of 'folk' music.

    C the process by which 'folk' music is created.

    D the unchanging nature of 'folk' music.

37 The writer says that certain people disapprove of some kinds of 'folk' music on the grounds that

    A it fails to exploit the music's true spirit.

    B it misrepresents the way their community lives.

    C it combines styles which do not sound good together.

    D it shows disrespect for the traditions of the music.

38 The writer repeats the word 'yes' near the beginning of the fourth paragraph to

    A underline that he really means what he is saying.

    B emphasise that contrasting beliefs co-exist within blues music.

    C anticipate the reader's questions about blues music.

    D convey his personal enthusiasm for blues music.

39 What does the writer imply about the 'common stock' of materials in blues music?

    A Some artists are less keen to make use of it than others.

    B Certain themes within it vary in popularity from time to time.

    C It is difficult to prove who wrote songs contained in it.

    D It is unlikely to maintain its popularity.

40 What does the writer imply about individuality in blues music?

    A It is more highly regarded than great musical ability.

    B It involves drawing on experiences unique to the particular performer.

    C It includes the expression of a surprising combination of emotions.

    D It is more likely to be conveyed vocally than by the playing of an instrument.

PAPER 2   WRITING (2 hours)

Part 1

You **must** answer this question. Write your answer in **300–350** words in an appropriate style.

1   You have read in a magazine the extracts below about studying history. The editor has asked readers for their opinions. You decide to write an article, responding to the points raised and expressing your own views.

> Studying history teaches us about cause and effect. It helps us understand how and why things happen and shows us patterns in human behaviour.

> Studying history is a waste of time. The past is no longer relevant to the present because our values have changed and we live our lives in a different way. We must look to the future, where we will find solutions to our problems.

Write your **article**.

Part 2

Write an answer to **one** of the questions **2–5** in this part. Write your answer in **300–350** words in an appropriate style.

---

2   You are involved in a project whose aim is to set up a group to run weekend activities for teenagers in your area. You have been asked to write a proposal to your local council so that they may consider giving you some funding. You should state why you wish to set up the group, what its aims are, and provide an outline of the proposed activities.

Write your **proposal**.

3   You have read an article in an international English magazine about the cultural significance of food. The magazine has invited readers to respond by writing a letter explaining the role of food in their own region or country. Readers are asked to focus on the role of food in daily life, customs and celebrations.

Write your **letter**. Do not write any addresses.

4   Your class is conducting a survey into different types of magazines that students read. Your tutor has asked you to write a review of a magazine which you enjoy reading, focusing on aspects such as the use of colour and pictures, design, interesting articles, appeal to the reader and value for money.

Write your **review**.

5   Based on your reading of **one** of these books, write on **one** of the following:

   (a)   Brian Moore: *The Colour of Blood*
   The Arts section of a popular magazine is planning a series of articles on thrillers entitled *You can't put them down ...* You have read *The Colour of Blood* and decide to submit an article which considers the many different aspects of the novel which make it impossible for the reader to put the book down.

   Write your **article**.

   (b)   L.P. Hartley: *The Go-Between*
   Write an essay for your tutor in which you briefly compare the characters of Lord Trimingham and Ted Burgess, and consider the way each of them behaves towards Leo.

   Write your **essay**.

   (c)   Chinua Achebe: *Things Fall Apart*
   An English language newspaper has asked its readers to recommend books for a feature entitled, *West Africa: A Passage in Time.* You decide to write a letter to the editor recommending *Things Fall Apart*, in which you describe the changes taking place in Okonkwo's world and the ways he responds to these changes.

   Write your **letter**. Do not write any addresses.

PAPER 3   USE OF ENGLISH (1 hour 30 minutes)

Part 1

For questions **1–15**, read the text below and think of the word which best fits each space. Use only **one** word in each space. There is an example at the beginning **(0)**.

Write your answers in CAPITAL LETTERS **on the separate answer sheet**.

Example: `0` `H` `A` `V` `E`

Budding Writers

What do Charles Dickens and Ernest Hemingway **(0)**......HAVE.... in common? The answer is that, along **(1)**............ many other famous novelists, their writing careers began on a local newspaper. Today, **(2)**............ its somewhat tarnished reputation, journalism still remains one of the few career paths open to the budding writer **(3)**............ his or her best to earn a living. **(4)**............ is more, many aspiring novelists are to be found biding their time on the staff of regional newspapers.

It is **(5)**............ exaggerating, however, to say that good writers are of **(6)**............ or no value to a newspaper **(7)**............ they do not know how to set about finding stories. Junior reporters have to devote hours to the cultivation of contacts who will **(8)**............ them supplied with the type of stories their readers have become **(9)**............ to seeing in print.

Newspapers also require a particular style. The graduate entrant to journalism, all of **(10)**............ experience and training is based on essay writing, may find the discipline required in writing a news report rather **(11)**............ daunting prospect. The philosophy of the newspaper is quite simple, **(12)**............ the fact that there are thousands of words competing **(13)**............ a limited number of columns. In addition, the average reader only spends at **(14)**............ twenty-five minutes reading a paper, so brevity is of **(15)**............ utmost importance.

Part 2

For questions **16–25**, read the text below. Use the word given in capitals at the end of some of the lines to form a word that fits in the space in the same line. There is an example at the beginning **(0)**.

Write your answers in CAPITAL LETTERS **on the separate answer sheet.**

Example: | 0 | C | O | L | O | U | R | F | U | L | | | | | | | | | |

Sir Walter Scott

Sir Walter Scott was the key figure in creating a **(0)** COLOURFUL. image of   **COLOUR**
Scotland's past, initially with his bestselling **(16)**............ poems, then with his   **NARRATE**
even more celebrated novels, the first of which was *Waverley*. It was published
anonymously in 1814 and, in subsequent years, its **(17)**............ were   **SUCCEED**
described as being 'by the author of *Waverley*', which accounts for the term
'Waverley novels'. Although Scott made no public **(18)**............ of his   **KNOWLEDGE**
(19)............ until 1827, the writer's identity was an open secret long before then.   **AUTHOR**
He wrote **(20)**............ quickly, and the first collected edition of the Waverley   **ORDINARY**
novels was published as early as 1819. A set of illustrations by Alexander
Nasmyth was produced for the second collected edition and these drawings were
used on the title pages.

Nasmyth has been called the father of landscape painting and, like
Walter Scott, he helped to **(21)**............ his country's romantic and   **POPULAR**
(22)............ scenery. The drawings were recently presented to the National   **PICTURE**
Library of Scotland, which now boasts a superb and **(23)**............ collection of   **RIVAL**
manuscripts and papers relating to Scott and his circle.

What is less well known about Sir Walter Scott is that after his **(24)**............ in   **BANKRUPT**
1826, his last years were spent in frantic literary activity to pay off all the
(25)............ to whom he owed money.   **CREDIT**

Part 3

For questions **26–31**, think of **one** word only which can be used appropriately in all three sentences. Here is an example **(0)**.

Example:

0 Some of the tourists are hoping to get compensation for the poor state of the hotel, and I think they have a very .... case.

There's no point in trying to wade across the river, the current is far too ....

If you're asking me which of the candidates should get the job, I'm afraid I don't have any .... views either way.

0	S	T	R	O	N	G											

Write **only** the missing word in CAPITAL LETTERS **on the separate answer sheet**.

---

26 The mountain .... is usually blocked by snow between March and December.

You cannot get into the military zone without a security ....

Rovers' captain sent a fantastic .... between two defenders to set up a scoring chance for the striker.

27 John accepted that his new position would .... a lot of hard work.

A red sky in the morning tends to .... bad weather is on the way.

I didn't .... to tell him, it just slipped out.

28 I had to wait some time to try on the trousers as all the changing rooms were ....

Once you've retired, why don't you look for a part-time job to keep yourself .... ?

It was five minutes before the start of the concert and very few seats were ....

29   The hotel manager wanted the builders to give him a better .... of the cost of the new leisure complex before he gave the go-ahead.

Our .... for the holiday is to set out on foot, then resort to public transport when we get tired.

I don't care what you say, she's not my .... of a good mother, allowing her children to roam the streets at that time of night!

30   The many coloured illustrations and diagrams are a particular .... of this dictionary.

Kathy's first job as a journalist was to write a .... about hairdressing for a local newspaper.

His intense blue eyes are his most striking physical ....

31   After .... dust in an attic for many years, the collection of paintings is now about to go on show to the public.

As he walked home, Boris was aware of storm clouds .... in the sky behind him.

The couple's 25th wedding anniversary provided a good opportunity for .... together all their old photographs in one large album.

Part 4

For questions **32–39**, complete the second sentence so that it has a similar meaning to the first sentence, using the word given. **Do not change the word given.** You must use between **three** and **eight** words, including the word given.

Here is an example **(0)**.

Example:

0 Do you mind if I watch you while you paint?

objection

Do you .... you while you paint?

0	*have any objection to my watching*

Write **only** the missing words **on the separate answer sheet**.

---

32 My two brothers don't trust each other at all.

complete

There's .... my two brothers.

33 In his autobiography, the famous singer did not mention how his first teacher had influenced him.

reference

In his autobiography, the famous singer .... of his first teacher.

34 If it rains, they will hold the concert indoors.

event

The concert .... rain.

35 It was a great surprise to us when Anna arrived punctually yesterday.

arrival

Anna took .... yesterday.

36 The thing I'd like most would be to see Igor again.

more

There's .... to see Igor again.

37 The judge said that it was only because of the woman's age he had not sent her to jail.

her

The judge said that had .... have sent the woman to jail.

38 As far as I'm aware, he's telling the truth.

suppose

I've .... he's lying.

39 The weather forecast says it will probably rain tonight.

threat

The weather forecast says .... tonight.

Part 5

For questions **40–44**, read the following texts about animals. For questions **40–43**, answer with a word or short phrase. You do not need to write complete sentences. For question **44**, write a summary according to the instructions given.

Write your answers to questions **40–44 on the separate answer sheet**.

Our attitudes to animals are marked by favouritism. Cats, dogs, horses and apes top the list; slugs, skunks, rats and mice come near the bottom. Favourite animals are like glossy magazines: chosen not for their intellect but their texture. Certain animals can be dressed in human costumes and sat down in some imaginary domestic scene. It helps if they have bright eyes and appealing fur. Rats and mice fail on most counts: their scuttling movements, lightless coat and raw pink tails mark them down for persecution. Favourite among the wild mammals of Britain is the badger who, like his cousin the bear, has a starring role in children's stories. In these tales, the badgers sit in their neatly buttoned trousers, sipping tea and discussing the ways of man, their common enemy. Immortalised by the enchantment of childhood, they become our imaginary companions. We carry them within us in a place of innocence where 'only man is vile'. As a result, the badger is now a legally 'protected' species – one which may not be harmed or disturbed. Sometimes at dusk, a badger scouts the pasture by our house, sniffing out its rodent prey. Seeing it so ruthlessly at work, however, I wonder why it is this animal which needs our protection, and not its victims. Indeed, in my view you do not protect wildlife by granting privileges to your favourites, but by seeing those favourites for what they are – an integral part of the natural food chain, equally crucial to its maintenance as any other.

40 Which word in the text is used to underline the fact that the badger is an effective hunter?

....

41 Which phrase is used in the text to emphasise that not all animals are treated fairly by environmental legislation?

....

For a million years people were hunters; for ten thousand years they were farmers; for the last one hundred years people in the west have been trying to deny all that, at least in terms of their relationship with animals. To an ever more urban population in the western world, animals are things, like the antiseptic plastic-wrapped packages of featherless chicken wings sold on a Styrofoam tray; or they are people, like the tea-drinking chimpanzees in a television commercial. The true character of animals and their meaning in the world, once common knowledge to the humans whose lives intertwined with theirs, is today lost in a miasma of human fantasies.

If the Industrial Revolution made animals into mere objects to be used as humans saw fit, the nature-worshipping counter-revolution that followed made them into objects of adoration to be revered. Wolves, the favourite villains of traditional fairy tales, are now ecological heroes, majestic symbols of the wild and freedom. Our favourite animal, as revealed in a survey of visitors to a well-known zoo, is the giant panda, typically described by zoo-goers as 'cute, cuddly, and adorable'. It's actually solitary, ill-tempered, and aggressive, but never mind.   line 16 Genuine understanding, which used to come from actual experience of the natural world, and which today could come from scientific studies of behaviour and ecology, is no match for such human preconceptions in a world where nature is viewed either as a factory or a theme park.

42   In your own words, explain what the example of the chimpanzees in the first paragraph illustrates.

   ....

43   In your own words, explain the meaning of the phrase 'but never mind' (line 16) in the context of the passage.

   ....

44   In a paragraph of **50–70** words, summarise **in your own words as far as possible** why people tend to like some animals more than others, using information from **both** texts. Write your summary **on the separate answer sheet**.

PAPER 4   LISTENING (40 minutes approximately)

Part 1

You will hear four different extracts. For questions **1–8**, choose the answer (**A**, **B** or **C**) which fits best according to what you hear. There are two questions for each extract.

Extract One

You hear part of a radio programme about science fiction films.

1 The speaker compares science fiction films with myths to make the point that they

    A have a universal appeal.
    B show people in a heroic light.
    C create an imaginary universe.

	1

2 According to the speaker, why did science fiction films begin to go out of fashion?

    A The films became more factual.
    B There was over-use of special effects.
    C Audiences were increasingly critical.

	2

Extract Two

You hear part of an interview with an expert on animal behaviour.

3 According to Dr Peters, in the past scientists were doubtful about the use of the term 'superorganism' because they felt

    A it did not reflect the complexity of the structure.
    B there was a limited need for such a term.
    C it was inherently misleading.

	3

4 Ant colonies are a good example of a superorganism because

    A they benefit from the social nature of ants.
    B they rely on individual ants doing different jobs.
    C they have a flexible structure.

	4

Extract Three

You hear part of a talk on the radio in which a novelist describes how she writes.

5 What is the novelist's opinion of writing thrillers?

    A   She finds the task of creating the plot complicated.
    B   She considers the actual process of writing them rather dull.
    C   She thinks the language she can use in a thriller is too limited.

	5

6 How does the novelist feel when she is writing the end of a book?

    A   surprised that everything has fallen into place
    B   excited at the thought of readers discovering her novel
    C   proud of having created another original work

	6

Extract Four

You hear part of a lecture about the history of clothing.

7 What aspect of clothing is being discussed?

    A   the importance of decoration
    B   the practicalities of fastening
    C   the social implications of fashion

	7

8 What is the speaker doing when she speaks?

    A   putting forward a possible explanation
    B   emphasising a historical detail
    C   illustrating the significance of fashion

	8

Part 2

You will hear part of a radio programme in which food historian Andrew Dalford talks about pepper, one of the commonest spices. For questions **9–17**, complete the sentences with a word or short phrase.

Andrew Dalford's recently published book about the history of spices is entitled

	9

The colour of the pepper is related to when the

	10	takes place.

In the past, dishonest dealers would add cheaper plant materials such as

	and		**11**	to sacks of pepper.

Andrew uses the term

	12	to describe the social importance of pepper throughout history.

Peppercorns could be used in financial transactions, like paying

	13	and clearing debts.

Together with ivory and

	14	, pepper was regarded as a luxury item in the Roman Empire.

In medicine, both pepper and

	15	were used to treat certain conditions.

Made into an ointment, pepper was used to treat irritated

	16	and to relieve pain.

Pepper in solution or as a powder was used to keep

	17	away.

Part 3

You will hear part of a radio discussion about graphology, the study of handwriting. For questions **18–22**, choose the answer (**A**, **B**, **C** or **D**) which fits best according to what you hear.

18 According to Richard, comments on a client's personality traits should only be made if the graphologist

   A   is sure that the sample of handwriting is genuine.
   B   is sure his results are supported by the rest of his team.
   C   can back up his initial findings with further evidence.
   D   can confirm his findings in different handwriting samples.

   | 18 |

19 What is Maria's view of the conclusions which graphologists arrive at?

   A   The rules of interpretation are not clear.
   B   The connections have not been proved.
   C   More detailed interpretation is needed.
   D   Research is needed into the way writing is taught.

   | 19 |

20 What, in Richard's view, is the key to an understanding of a client's personality?

   A   the way in which the client learnt to write
   B   the variations in the client's individual letters
   C   the way the client's handwriting has developed
   D   the influence of current trends on the client's handwriting

   | 20 |

21 According to Richard, some businesses with North American links

   A   use graphology reluctantly in recruitment.
   B   are unwilling to disclose that they use graphology.
   C   are sceptical about the value of graphology.
   D   are trading more successfully because of graphology.

   | 21 |

22 What does Maria conclude about the use of graphology?

   A   It has become a source of discontent.
   B   It is used by few serious psychologists.
   C   Its educational value has not been proved.
   D   It is not appropriate for use as a recruitment tool.

   | 22 |

Part 4

You will hear two friends, Dominic and Sue, talking about formality in the workplace. For questions **23–28**, decide whether the opinions are expressed by only one of the speakers, or whether the speakers agree.

Write: **S**   for Sue,
          D   for Dominic,
or   **B**   for Both, where they agree.

23   Today's technology removes the need for open-plan offices. | | 23 |

24   Company policy determines the level of formality required when dealing with others. | | 24 |

25   Dressing casually for work is not always appropriate. | | 25 |

26   There are similarities in attitude towards dress between school and the workplace. | | 26 |

27   Some people need guidance as to what to wear. | | 27 |

28   Clothes can create artificial differences between work colleagues. | | 28 |

PAPER 5   SPEAKING (19 minutes)

There are two examiners. One (the interlocutor) conducts the test, providing you with the necessary materials and explaining what you have to do. The other examiner (the assessor) will be introduced to you, but then takes no further part in the interaction.

Part 1 (3 minutes)

The interlocutor first asks you and your partner a few questions which focus on information about yourselves and personal opinions.

Part 2 (4 minutes)

In this part of the test you and your partner are asked to talk together. The interlocutor places a set of pictures on the table in front of you. There may be only one picture in the set or as many as seven pictures. This stimulus provides the basis for a discussion. The interlocutor first asks an introductory question which focuses on two of the pictures (or in the case of a single picture, on aspects of the picture). After about a minute, the interlocutor gives you both a decision-making task based on the same set of pictures.

The pictures for Part 2 are on pages C2–C3 of the colour section.

Part 3 (12 minutes)

You are each given the opportunity to talk for two minutes, to comment after your partner has spoken and to take part in a more general discussion.

The interlocutor gives you a card with a question written on it and asks you to talk about it for two minutes. After you have spoken, your partner is first asked to comment and then the interlocutor asks you both another question related to the topic on the card. This procedure is repeated, so that your partner receives a card and speaks for two minutes, you are given an opportunity to comment and a follow-up question is asked.

Finally, the interlocutor asks some further questions, which leads to a discussion on a general theme related to the subjects already covered in Part 3.

The cards for Part 3 are on pages C5 and C10 of the colour section.

Test 2

PAPER 1 READING (1 hour 30 minutes)

Part 1

For questions **1–18**, read the three texts below and decide which answer (**A**, **B**, **C** or **D**) best fits each gap.

Mark your answers **on the separate answer sheet**.

Professional sport

When I talk about practice, I mean something individual. If you look at professional golfers or tennis players, you will observe that practice **(1)** …. the basis of their preparation for tournaments. Of course it does, **(2)** …. these are individual sports. Training is simply doing the physical work necessary to be sufficiently fit, but practice entails making an analysis of one's game, locating its weak points, and working to **(3)** …. them. If your opponent keeps winning points by serving high to your backhand, there's no place to hide; you either have to **(4)** …. the weakness, or you'll keep losing to him. He'll exploit your weaknesses mercilessly.

Part of what is fascinating, and slightly repellent, about sport lies in that curious inversion of values **(5)** …. much that we admire in ordinary life – humility, compassion, unwillingness to take advantage of the weakness of others – is reversed on the field of play. Professional sport is all about winning. And, within **(6)** …. the more you practise (and the more you train), the better your chances of doing so.

1 A lays	**B** composes	**C** enacts	**D** forms
2 A albeit	**B** for	**C** as with	**D** let alone
3 A eradicate	**B** rid	**C** wipe	**D** extinguish
4 A alter	**B** square	**C** reform	**D** rectify
5 A insofar	**B** whereby	**C** thereof	**D** hence
6 A due	**B** sense	**C** reason	**D** merit

Introduction to a magazine feature

Are your cupboards bursting at the seams, your bag full of unwanted receipts, sweet wrappers and chewed up pens? Do you often spend ages searching for keys, or telephone numbers **(7)** .... down on the backs of envelopes? If the answer is 'yes', then worry no more. The order and calm you long for is nearer than you think. Just follow our guide to decluttering your life.

It's difficult to think clearly or creatively, to relax or **(8)** .... , if you live amongst piles of junk. Clutter has a way of controlling us. When our environment is in a **(9)** ...., our minds can also feel disordered. When rubbish is allowed to **(10)** .... up, and stagnate, a combination of frustration, confusion and lethargy **(11)** .... ; we can feel stuck and unsure of our direction. Clearing out unused and unwanted **(12)** .... allows us to focus more clearly. Try for yourself and see.

7 A jotted	**B** penned	**C** doodled	**D** etched
8 A unfold	**B** unleash	**C** unload	**D** unwind
9 A dump	**B** chaos	**C** mess	**D** tip
10 A clog	**B** build	**C** stock	**D** grow
11 A holds on	**B** stands out	**C** joins up	**D** sets in
12 A features	**B** items	**C** matters	**D** entities

Problem staff

The issue of problem staff in restaurants covers a multitude of sins. Usually poor service comes **(13)** .... to the behaviour of an individual employee, but it's also the restaurant's responsibility. Why should restaurant managers tolerate bad attitudes? When you do get a less than helpful waiter, it's tempting to suggest to the manager or owner that the individual concerned might be better employed elsewhere – not in the service industry, perhaps. **(14)** .... are they're already aware of such 'attitude issues' and tolerate bad behaviour for reasons best **(15)** .... to themselves. This is when it's worth remembering that a service charge isn't mandatory. **(16)** .... them where it hurts – in the **(17)** .... packet, and eventually they might **(18)** .... the message.

13 A over	**B** along	**C** up	**D** down
14 A Possibilities	**B** Chances	**C** Eventualities	**D** Prospects
15 A renowned	**B** familiar	**C** known	**D** acknowledged
16 A Tap	**B** Knock	**C** Hit	**D** Strike
17 A pay	**B** salary	**C** wages	**D** earnings
18 A catch	**B** get	**C** take	**D** grasp

Part 2

You are going to read four extracts which are all concerned in some way with the natural world. For questions **19–26**, choose the answer (**A**, **B**, **C** or **D**) which you think fits best according to the text.

Mark your answers **on the separate answer sheet**.

The Sea

I recently asked the Japanese photographer Hiroshi Sugimoto why he had continued, from the 1980s to the present, to photograph the ostensibly monotonous subject of rippling oceans. Sugimoto's explanation was surprising; it went far beyond aquatic aesthetics and into the realm of deep time. He pointed out that the sea was essentially the one thing on our earth that has remained virtually unaffected in several millennia. Since antediluvian times, people have stared at the endless masses of dark salt water that cover seven-tenths of our world and, invariably, felt small, solitary, transient and awestruck.

The history of marine art is the story of a passage from religious awe and darkness to a world in which the sea has become ineffable and impervious to representation with only mavericks continuing to engage with its essential opacity. It's a long way from the rolling oceans that menaced the British painter Turner's ships, to the candied, glitter-dusted waves in the recent works of Kate Bright or the glassy, untroubled waters that appear frozen in Sugimoto's exquisite parade of monochromatic images. But then, although the seas are approximately the same as they ever were, it's a different world on land.

19 With his question to Hiroshi Sugimoto, the writer implies that

    A Sugimoto's work has become outdated.
    B there have been few changes in the work of marine artists.
    C there is little of interest in the sea to depict.
    D Sugimoto's work fails to show the variable nature of the oceans.

20 According to the writer, the recent developments in marine art show that

    A the true nature of the sea is difficult to capture.
    B the sea is widely regarded as a benevolent force.
    C artists understand better how light affects water.
    D unconventional artists have become more influential.

The Walk

During the first hour or so Clive felt, despite his optimism, the unease of outdoor solitude wrap itself around him. Now and then he glanced over his shoulder. He knew this feeling well because he often hiked alone. There was always a reluctance to be overcome. It was an act of will, a tussle with instinct, to keep walking away from the nearest people, from shelter, warmth and help. A sense of scale habituated to the daily perspectives of rooms and streets was suddenly affronted by a colossal emptiness. His shrinking spirit and all his basic inclinations told him that it was foolish and unnecessary to keep on, that he was making a mistake.

He kept on because the shrinking and apprehension were precisely the conditions – the sickness – from which he sought release, and proof that his daily grind – crouching over that piano for hours every day – had reduced him to a cringing state. He would be large again, and unafraid. Soon human meaning would be bleached from the rocks, the landscape would assume its beauty and draw him in; the unimaginable age of the mountains and the fine mesh of living things that lay across them would remind him that he was part of this order and insignificant within it, and he would be set free.

21 Clive knew from experience that he would

   A regret his lack of preparation for the walk.
   B have problems with his sense of direction.
   C initially feel threatened by the open landscape.
   D need to walk alone in order to prove his independence.

22 Clive continued on his walk because his aim was to achieve

   A a greater sense of his own importance.
   B a change in his perspective.
   C a feeling of isolation.
   D greater creativity.

South Georgia

Visually and emotionally, the island of South Georgia overwhelms. At first glance, it resembles the far South Atlantic branch of a fantastic zoo: a profusion of captivating animals that quickly transforms even the most discriminating observer into a raving anthropomorphic. Its conglomeration of dark peaks, white glaciers, snow and ice, green tussock grasses and mosses, brown mud and bogs and colourful animals suggests no landscape that the masters' brushes have rendered. Its mountains have been dubbed the 'Alps of the Southern Ocean', and its surrounding waters remain among the world's richest.

The resident human population is zero, the penguin, seabird and seal population is boundless, and the resulting minority status for human beings does wonders for one's psyche. This far-flung outpost **line 13** lacks plane trails in the sky, rock music in the streets, garbage in the landscape, and blathering politicians immersed in inconsequential minutiae. In their stead, one's ears tune quickly to the whistling and calling king penguins, the bleating, growling fur seals, and the belching and grunting elephant seals. South Georgia is for contemplative types, offering refuge from the schisms of daily existence on our crowded planet.

23 The writer implies that the wildlife in South Georgia

- **A** has great appeal.
- **B** is limited in type.
- **C** is drab in appearance.
- **D** has unusual characteristics.

24 According to the second paragraph, what 'does wonders for one's psyche'? (line 13)

- **A** the presence of wild animals
- **B** the scarcity of people
- **C** the absence of noise
- **D** the lack of conflict

Nature and Poetry

A poetic appreciation of nature and our relationships with it remains more or less excluded from serious debate and decision-making about nature conservation on the grounds that it is merely subjective and emotional. Nature poetry seems cursed to fall between two stools: it is either written off as a narrow, escapist activity disconnected from reality, or it is put on an elitist pedestal and viewed as a source of inspiration, precious but separate from 'real' life.

A generation of British schoolchildren that has grown up with the writing of the poets Seamus Heaney and Ted Hughes knows this is rubbish. Even poetry which reaches into the cosmos can be grounded in the particular, the vernacular, the everyday – and be as rigorously observed as scientific investigation. Despite the hold that science has over our culture, people all over the country are reading, writing and performing nature poetry without apologising for their sense of wonder. Romantics, ecofeminists, spiritual ecologists, shamen, traditional naturalists, environmentalists – the whole spectrum of people who take nature as their primal source – are developing a new aesthetic of the wild, and inspiring people concerned with the environment. Sure, there's some slushy sentimental twaddle in there, but why use that as an excuse to discriminate against nature poetry in general? It's high time that the supremacy of science was challenged; who better than poets to lead the onslaught?

25 The writer believes that a poetic view of the natural world

   A is rightly held to be intellectually exclusive.
   B represents a form of artistic escape from the real world.
   C is unfairly considered inappropriate to rational discussion of the environment.
   D provides practical insight into the real world.

26 Which of the following statements best summarises the writer's view of science?

   A Scientific methodology is inappropriate to the study of nature.
   B Science is stifling creative thought.
   C Scientific discoveries are irrelevant to most people.
   D Scientific values are over-dominant in today's society.

Part 3

You are going to read an extract from a newspaper article about a trip to Alaska. Seven paragraphs have been removed from the extract. Choose from the paragraphs **A–H** the one which fits each gap (**27–33**). There is one extra paragraph which you do not need to use.

Mark your answers **on the separate answer sheet**.

How I Baked in Alaska

Something was missing when Nigel Worthington landed in mid-winter Alaska.

I'd come to Alaska to watch preparations for the Iditarod, the longest, most gruelling dog-sled race in the world. And when it comes to setting off on a trip through the sub-Arctic wilderness in mid-January, one doesn't like to take chances. Consequently, there wasn't much in the way of winter wear that I hadn't packed: long fleecy underwear, eiderdown jackets, and several layers of socks. I even had goggles, a facemask and a new beard grown specially for the occasion. I was wearing just about the lot when I waddled off Alaska Airlines Flight 93 from London to Anchorage.

27	

'This is where we skate,' my driver said listlessly as, on the way into town, we drove past a melted pond, its surface dancing with falling rain. 'This is where we snowshoe,' she gloomily intoned a minute later, pointing at an open expanse in the forest. It was a brown, churned-up bog of mud. 'And this is where we cross-country ski,' she said, her voice close to cracking with emotion now, as she indicated what was once a trail running beside the road. Not only was the grass and moss there exposed – it was green and appeared to be growing.

28	

With this in mind, I was headed for Winterlake Lodge, checkpoint number six on the 1,100 mile-long Iditarod Trail and home of wilderness guide Carl Dixon who, with his wife Kirsten, an award-winning chef, keeps 26 sled-dogs. With a little supervision, he allows city folk like me to test their mettle on the runners of a dog-sled.

29	

But it wasn't to be. While my isolated, roadless, destination lay far inland and was a good deal colder than coastal Anchorage – there was snow on the ground up there – unsettled conditions and poor visibility ruled out any prospect of flying that day. For hours, I sat by a loaded De Haviland Beaver waiting for a break in the weather until finally, with the short Alaskan day closing in, we gave up the ghost.

30	

After all, the sprawling, modern city of 260,000 can seem a little short on charm. Although almost half the state's population lives there, Alaskans do not see the malls, high-rises and multiplex cinemas as having much to do with the land they live in. Perched on the edge of a vast wilderness, Anchorage, they like to say, is 'just 20 minutes from Alaska'.

31	

But there was not a flake of snow to be seen on the streets. Already the Klondike 300, a qualifying race for the Iditarod, had been cancelled for lack of snow. Now the city fathers, panicky, had ordered the stockpiling of up-country snow reserves that could be spread on the street on the day of the race. The situation was desperate.

32	

Free at last to take in the sights, I zipped up my thermal jacket and ventured forth. Disconcertingly, the first person I passed was a window-washer working in a short-sleeved, hibiscus-red Hawaiian shirt. But by the time I'd strolled along the main drag three or four times, I was beginning to feel a little less conspicuous. In the relative chill of early evening, one or two locals even seemed to be wearing gloves.

33

It was not the little one that handled Beavers though, but the big one where I had arrived. Leaving aside for the moment the vast pack of unused winter clothes I

dragged back to London, what got me hottest under the collar about my trip to the Great White North was seeing the next day's weather report for Alaska. Under clear skies, temperatures were dropping; snow was on the way.

A In anticipation of just such a challenge, I had read the hairy-chested prose of Jack London and listened to the rough-and-ready goldrush doggerel of Robert Service. In my mind, I had mushed the snowy frozen trails of Alaska all the way from Skagway to the Yukon River. Like the keenest of huskies, I was straining at the leash.

B Alaskans, it seems, get pretty heated up about any subject you care to name, and this one was no exception. The opinions in the airport bar were extreme and unpredictable; I felt lucky to get out in one piece.

C I couldn't have been less prepared for the freakish conditions that greeted me. The skies were so filled with mist and rain that I was denied any glimpse of the great mountain chain that soars skyward just behind the city. The air was so balmy that I couldn't even see my own breath.

D How frustrating, then, to be a whole season away. It didn't help that, from my window, I could see the bronze-sculpted statue of Balto, the most famous lead dog in the Iditarod's 28-year history. It is here that the race begins each year, with more than 50 teams of sled-dogs straining in the traces before they fly round the corner and into the wild, only to reappear many days later in distant Nome.

E By noon the next day I had caught the mood. With Carl telephoning me regularly with weather updates, I couldn't even go out and explore. As the hours ticked slowly by, and visibility dropped even further, I got to wondering how Alaskan trappers and miners hold out for entire winters in the lonely wilderness. By four, when Dixon phoned to say he was again calling it a day, I was climbing the walls – and I had cable television!

F One consolation was that I got to check into the Anchorage Hotel. It is among the oldest buildings in the city and one of the few to have survived the powerful earthquake which rocked the region in 1964. There was a slight tilt to the floor in the corridor, but I liked the place all the more for it, it added character.

G I will not labour you with a dreary account of my mental deterioration the next day as the prospects of onward travel grew ever remoter. Suffice it to say that when Carl told me that afternoon that the flight was in doubt yet again, I headed for the airport.

H For in spite of their tendency to fly to Hawaii for winter breaks, Alaskans are really fond of winter. Never had they seen such unseasonal mildness and I shared their dismay. Although a rank beginner, I had set my heart on having a go at dog-sledding myself.

Part 4

You are going to read an extract from a novel. For questions **34–40**, choose the answer (**A, B, C** or **D**) which you think fits best according to the text.

Mark your answers **on the separate answer sheet**.

SAM AND HIS FATHER

Sam pushed open the front door. His father, Mike, was sitting in his chair, watching daytime TV. 'Do you want to watch this?' Sam asked pointedly. The yammering faces of the talk show filled the screen with stories of outrage, attended by resentment and rancour.

'I thought maybe we could talk,' Sam added.

He moved his father's stick from beside his chair so that he could pull his own seat closer, partly blocking out the TV screen. The result was that they sat almost knee to knee. Sam could have reached and taken Mike's hand between his own, but he didn't. They had never gone in for touching, not since Sam was a little boy.

Mike's response was to aim the remote and lower the volume by a couple of decibels. Then he turned to look his son in the face.

'I didn't qualify,' Sam said.

There were two, three beats of silence.

Mike rubbed the corner of his mouth with a horny thumb. 'Huh?'

'I ran in Pittsburgh last week. It was the Olympic Trials.'

Sam had been training for the City of Pittsburgh Marathon ever since the USA Track & Field international competition committee had announced that the Olympic men's marathon team would once again be decided, as it had been for more than thirty years, by a single race. And for Sam it had been one of those days when the running machine had kept stalling and finally quit. He didn't suffer many of them, but when the machinery did let him down it was usually to do with the weight of expectation binding and snagging. His father's expectations, specifically. Sam was fully aware of the dynamic between them, but awareness didn't change it or diminish the effects. Even now.

'I didn't know.'

The old man's face didn't give much away. He just went on looking at Sam, waiting for him to explain himself.

It was so characteristic, Sam thought, that he wouldn't have known or found out about the run even though his son was a contender for the US Olympic team. But it was equally characteristic, Sam acknowledged, that he hadn't told his father about Pittsburgh. He had qualified for the trials by running a time better than two hours twenty in a national championship race and he had called Mike immediately afterwards to tell him so.

'That's pretty good,' had been the entire response.

In adulthood, Sam had trained himself not to resent or rise to his father's lack of enthusiasm. It's the way he is, he reasoned. He wanted me to do one thing and I did another. But even so, that time Mike had seemed particularly grudging. And so he had not told him anything more about the big race beforehand, or called him with the bad news once it was over. Instead, he had waited a week and then come down to visit the old man. He had played various versions of this scene in his head, giving Mike lines to express commiseration, or encouragement for next time, or plain sympathy – but the most cheerless scenario had been closest to reality.

Mike was neither surprised nor sympathetic, he was just disappointed. As he had been plenty of times before. The pattern was set now.

'So what happened?' Mike asked at last.

Sam caught himself shrugging and tried to stop it. 'I was fit enough and I felt good on the start. I don't know. I just couldn't make it work.'

Mike went on looking at him, saying nothing.

'There's always the next Olympics.' Sam smiled, thinking within himself: It should be the other way round. You should be saying that to me.

'I was looking forward to you bringing home that gold.' Mike nodded to the mantel, as if there were a space there, among the pictures of mountains and bearded men, that was bereaved of his son's Olympic medal.

'I'd have been happy enough just to go to the Olympics and represent my country. It never was just about winning, Dad,' Sam said patiently.

'No.'

The monosyllable was a taunt, expertly flicked, that dug into Sam like the barb of a fish-hook.

It's the way he is, Sam reminded himself. It's because he's bitter about his own life. And he's entitled to a grouse this time. He would have been proud of me if I'd made it, so it's understandable he should feel the opposite way now.

'I'm sorry I didn't make it this time. It was tough for me as well. But I won't stop running. It means a lot to me.'

'Keep at it while you still can,' Mike agreed. 'You're lucky.' Do you want me to say I'm sorry for that, as well? Sam wondered.

Mike had already turned his gaze over his son's shoulder, back towards the jeering audience on the television. The volume went up again.

34 When Sam sat down,

    A he made sure that he didn't sit too close to the TV screen.
    B his father made it clear that he didn't want Sam to touch him.
    C he did not feel that it would be natural for him to hold his father's hand.
    D a feeling that he had had as a child came back to him.

35 Sam felt that his failure in the race in Pittsburgh

    A proved that his relationship with his father had not changed.
    B was something that his father would have considered predictable.
    C was probably more due to physical than psychological causes.
    D highlighted the unfairness of the selection policy for the Olympics.

36 Before going to visit his father, Sam had

    A worried about some of the things he was going to say.
    B been too hopeful when imagining what would happen.
    C tried to forget how disappointed his father would be.
    D rejected a number of ways of handling the situation.

37 When Sam told his father what had happened in the race in Pittsburgh, Sam

    A was aware of the absence of words of encouragement from his father.
    B was determined to give the impression that he didn't feel very bad about it.
    C found it hard to understand why his father had so little to say.
    D made it clear that he did not feel it had been all his own fault.

38 When the subject of an Olympic medal was mentioned,

    A Sam was puzzled by his father's response.
    B his father's mood seemed to change.
    C his father made it clear to Sam that he disliked Sam's attitude to winning.
    D Sam realised that his father was concealing his true feelings from him.

39 At the end of the conversation, Sam felt that his father

    A hadn't been listening to him properly.
    B resented the fact that Sam could continue running.
    C enjoyed complaining about things.
    D should have been more consistent in his attitudes.

40 Which of the following best sums up the relationship between Sam and his father?

    A Sam's father actually liked him more than he was able to show.
    B Sam was rather confused as to why his father took such little interest in him.
    C Sam's father unintentionally caused him misery.
    D Sam generally tried not to think too badly of his father.

PAPER 2   WRITING (2 hours)

Part 1

You **must** answer this question. Write your answer in **300–350** words in an appropriate style.

---

1 You have read the two extracts below in class. Your tutor has asked you to write an essay discussing the topic *Computers – our best friend or worst enemy,* responding to the points raised and expressing your own views.

> Computers are the greatest invention ever. We have access to information on an incredible scale. We can also contact people anywhere in the world. There are endless possibilities.

> Computer technology is creating a society that is anti-social and lazy. The time will come when we will not need to use our brains for anything because the computer will provide us with all the answers. The consequences are frightening.

Write your **essay**.

Part 2

Write an answer to **one** of the questions **2–5** in this part. Write your answer in **300–350** words in an appropriate style.

---

2 The Tourist Board in your area has decided to produce a publication called 'Travelling on a Small Budget'. You work for the Tourist Board and have been asked to write a report for the brochure, explaining the advantages of your region in terms of cheap ways to travel around, places to stay and activities for visitors.

Write your **report**.

3 A magazine has invited readers to send in articles with the title 'My Ideal Home'. You decide to write an **article** in which you describe the structure and furnishings of your ideal home. You should discuss how this choice reflects your personality and consider what we can learn about people from the type of home they live in and the way they furnish it.

Write your **article**.

4 An international magazine has been running a series of articles on fame and the fascination that there is with famous people and their celebrity status. Write a letter to the magazine describing your country's media coverage of famous people and how you think that coverage affects their lives.

Write your **letter**. Do not write any addresses.

5 Based on your reading of **one** of these books, write on **one** of the following:

   (a) Brian Moore: *The Colour of Blood*
   You have recommended that *The Colour of Blood* is chosen as a suitable book for discussion by your reading group. However, the secretary of the group is concerned that the title of the book may give some readers a misleading impression of what it is about. You have been asked to write a report recommending the book and explaining the significance of the title.

   Write your **report**.

   (b) L.P. Hartley: *The Go-Between*
   You have had a class discussion on the importance of the opening lines in novels. Your tutor has asked you to write an essay on how effectively the first line of *The Go-Between* 'The past is a foreign country: they do things differently there' establishes the theme of the novel.

   Write your **essay**.

   (c) Chinua Achebe: *Things Fall Apart*
   Your reading group has asked members to write reviews of books which feature significant relationships between parents and children. You decide to write a review of *Things Fall Apart*, referring in particular to the relationship between Okonkwo and the children in his household, and focusing on what these relationships reveal about Okonkwo's character. You should include at least **two** of the following: Nwoye, Obiageli, Ezinma, or Ikemefuna.

   Write your **review**.

PAPER 3   USE OF ENGLISH (1 hour 30 minutes)

Part 1

For questions **1–15**, read the text below and think of the word which best fits each space. Use only **one** word in each space. There is an example at the beginning **(0)**.

Write your answers in CAPITAL LETTERS **on the separate answer sheet**.

Example: **0** | O | U | R |

Nothing's New In Medicine

Throughout the ages, disease has stalked **(0)**......OUR....... species. Prehistoric humans must quickly have learnt **(1)**............ could be eaten without danger, and how to avoid plants that could **(2)**............ about illness. They found leaves, berries and the bark of different trees that could actually heal wounds and cure the sick, and **(3)**............ soon became a special skill to understand natural medicine.

Ever **(4)**............ the dawn of history, medicine men and wise women have always been expert in treating diseases and have dispensed medicine with ritual and magic. **(5)**............ trial and error they discovered treatments for almost **(6)**............ affliction prevalent at the time. The precious recipes for preparations which could relieve pain, stop fits, sedate or stimulate were **(7)**............ down from generation to generation, **(8)**............ there was **(9)**............ exact understanding of the way in **(10)**............ the medicines worked. Nevertheless, **(11)**............ the power of these primitive medicines, generations were still ravaged by disease.

(12)............ the last 150 years, scientists and doctors, **(13)**............ work has focused on these early medicines, have learnt that their power derived **(14)**............ certain chemicals which were found in herbal remedies or could be synthesised in the laboratory. In just **(15)**............ a way, advances in modern medicine continue, aided by the discoveries made centuries ago by our ancestors.

Part 2

For questions **16–25**, read the text below. Use the word given in capitals at the end of some of the lines to form a word that fits in the space in the same line. There is an example at the beginning **(0)**.

Write your answers in CAPITAL LETTERS **on the separate answer sheet**.

Example: | **0** | E | F | F | E | C | T | I | V | E | | | | | | |

Power Naps

Power napping is an **(0)**..E̶F̶F̶E̶C̶T̶I̶V̶E̶.. and under-used tool. It is a quick, intense   **EFFECT**

sleep which **(16)**............ improves alertness. These naps are especially useful   **DRAMA**

for those whose sleep is constrained by a **(17)**............ schedule: for example,   **DEMAND**

mothers of small children or travelling business **(18)**............ . However, the   **EXECUTE**

conditions must be right and practice is required for maximum effect.

Power naps should be short, between ten and twenty-five minutes, to prevent

(19)............ on awakening. Some people believe it is impossible to fall asleep   **ORIENTATE**

in such a short time, but **(20)**............ of the habit is simply a question of   **ACQUIRE**

practice. At the **(21)**............ , it is more important to relax for a while than   **OUT**

actually fall asleep.

Power napping is not a good idea if you find it difficult to wake up at the

(22)............ time or have problems sleeping at night after a power nap in the   **DESIGN**

day. The kind of dozing that can **(23)**............ a sensation of overwhelming   **COMPANY**

(24)............ is not a true power nap, but a desperate attempt to compensate   **SLEEP**

for a poor sleep routine.

However, with practice, you will find that power naps can lead to a welcome

(25)............ of your performance when you need it most.   **ENHANCE**

Part 3

For questions **26–31**, think of **one** word only which can be used appropriately in all three sentences. Here is an example **(0)**.

Example:

0 Some of the tourists are hoping to get compensation for the poor state of the hotel, and I think they have a very .... case.

There's no point in trying to wade across the river, the current is far too ....

If you're asking me which of the candidates should get the job, I'm afraid I don't have any .... views either way.

0 | S | T | R | O | N | G | | | | | | | | | | | |

Write **only** the missing word in CAPITAL LETTERS **on the separate answer sheet**.

---

26 The trains are still .... despite the snow.

My nose has been .... all week because of this awful cold.

The project had to be completed by July and unfortunately we were .... short of time.

27 The quickest way to get back to the hotel is to .... across the meadows.

The newspapers are predicting that the government is going to .... interest rates next week.

As the play was in danger of being too long, the producer decided to .... part of the second act.

28 Hotels tend to .... their prices in the summer season.

We're hoping that the show we're putting on next month will .... a lot of money for charity.

The advertising campaign ought to .... the profile of the company.

29 Susan Moore is a world .... on ancient civilisations.

Only the treasurer has the .... to sign cheques.

Many schools in Britain are financed by a local .... in conjunction with central government funding.

30 Your work has not been up to standard in the last three months, but we are prepared to let you make a .... start.

Write the report today while the events are still .... in your mind.

You will find that Professor Stanton has an entirely .... approach to this problem.

31 The TV reporter gave a full .... of the run-up to the election.

You need to take the family's views into .... before you decide where to go on holiday.

Please don't make a fuss on my ....

Part 4

For questions **32–39**, complete the second sentence so that it has a similar meaning to the first sentence, using the word given. **Do not change the word given**. You must use between **three** and **eight** words, including the word given.

Here is an example **(0)**.

Example:

0 Do you mind if I watch you while you paint?

objection

Do you .... you while you paint?

0	*have any objection to my watching*

Write **only** the missing words **on the separate answer sheet**.

---

32 My sister needed more than three hours to finish her homework last night.

over

It .... her homework last night.

33 I couldn't find a parking space this morning.

anywhere

I was .... to park this morning.

34 I don't intend to wait here all morning.

intention

I .... here all morning.

35   The two children began to argue fiercely about who had damaged the bicycle.

broke

A .... the two children about who had damaged the bicycle.

36   I admire her business ability but not the way she manages her staff.

dislike

Much .... the way she manages her staff.

37   Janet seems to me to be very happy in her new job.

aware

As .... Janet is very happy in her new job.

38   A computer breakdown was blamed for the delayed dispatch of the brochures.

reason

A computer breakdown was given .... in dispatching the brochures.

39   The sequel to the best seller was a great disappointment to the public.

live

The sequel to the best seller .... of the public.

Part 5

For questions **40–44**, read the following texts on genealogy. For questions **40–43**, answer with a word or short phrase. You do not need to write complete sentences. For question **44**, write a summary according to the instructions given.

Write your answers to questions **40–44 on the separate answer sheet**.

Originally transmitted orally, genealogies or family histories were a way of tracing the descent of a race or people through its ruling dynasty from a figure or deity **line 2** from whom the race took its name. They were often purely speculative about the earliest generations because of the artificial purpose they served – to show continuity from an illustrious ancestor to the present day. As well as tracing the origins of a race, the pedigree or family tree bound its members in a close sense of kinship, reinforced by its recitation on ceremonial occasions, normally in a **line 7** poetic or chronicle form that was easy to memorise. The Ashanti and Yoruba tribes of West Africa have their own hereditary tribal historian whose function it is to preserve these genealogical traditions, while in Scotland, the 'Lord Lyon King of Arms' remains the genealogist for all the clans.

A Scottish clan is composed of the descendants of an actual or mythical ancestor, the chief of the clan being the senior male descendant in direct line. Each clan was originally organised on a territorial basis, which helped the family historian to discover at least which part of the country his antecedents stemmed from. For a clan member, a knowledge of his own genealogy and that of his chief was an integral part of his life, although no written record of it might exist. Family celebrations were the occasion for the recital of pedigrees to stress the unity and history of the line.

40 To what does 'its' refer? (line 7)

....

41 Which phrase in the second paragraph echoes the idea of 'figure or deity' in line 2?

....

The need for genealogy arose from people's yearning to know more about their ancestry. For a long time legends were enough, but eventually, the desire to find the objective truth concerning the actual ancestors was to exert itself. The personification of history, which was the original purpose of genealogy, is still its greatest fascination, all the more so now that it is (or should be) dealing in   **line 5** scientifically proven facts. Tracing the history of one family is an admirable way of learning history. The reflection of wars and great national events on a set of individual families can sometimes tell one much more than the sweeping generalisations of a few politico-economic historians. Similarly, how much deeper an understanding of social history can be derived by reading the plain facts about families without having them interpreted and analysed by a sociologist.

The growth of genealogy took place as nations established themselves with modes of government and legal systems. Royal genealogies, as set out in the chronicle books, were obviously of the utmost importance in deciding the succession of royal families. The desire to assert the privileges of an aristocracy by birth was a powerful factor in Roman and Ancient Greek times and in the development of genealogy throughout history. Inheritance was the heart of the hereditary principle and in this context genealogists were able to trace the historical development of a surname by establishing when it had first been recorded. In settling disputes as to the inheritance of property, genealogy came into its own.

42 Explain in your own words what the writer considers to be 'greatest fascination' of genealogy. (line 5)

....

43 Which phrase in the text indicates that the writer is critical of a certain profession?

....

44 In a paragraph of **50–70** words, summarise **in your own words as far as possible** the importance of genealogy throughout history, using information from **both** texts. Write your summary **on the separate answer sheet**.

PAPER 4 LISTENING (40 minutes approximately)

Part 1

You will hear four different extracts. For questions **1–8**, choose the answer (**A**, **B** or **C**) which fits best according to what you hear. There are two questions for each extract.

Extract One

You hear the beginning of a radio programme about anger.

1 What does the speaker say about losing your temper?

   A It's easier for adults to restrain themselves.
   B It's made worse by the pressures of modern living.
   C It's difficult for some people to acknowledge.

   1

2 How does the speaker suggest we feel after we have regained our temper?

   A ashamed at our loss of control
   B determined to avoid repeating the incident
   C unaware of how foolish we appeared

   2

Extract Two

You hear part of a discussion in which a writer, Michael Holmes, is talking about the difference between biographies and autobiographies.

3 According to Michael Holmes, the writers of autobiographies tend to

   A reveal information about themselves unintentionally.
   B provide a fuller picture of their lives than a biographer can.
   C get the facts right about the details of their careers.

   3

4 What is Michael Holmes' attitude to the rock star, Frank Silver?

   A He finds Frank overprotective of his family.
   B He criticises Frank's obsession with his image.
   C He is surprised by Frank's desire to get the facts right.

   4

Extract Three

You hear an environmentalist talking about alien plant species.

5 The speaker is concerned about alien plant species because their presence

   A   reduces the overall number of different plants.
   B   encourages the introduction of harmful diseases.
   C   changes the climatic conditions in certain areas.

5

6 According to the speaker, why were alien plant species introduced?

   A   to eliminate certain insect pests
   B   to make an area visually attractive
   C   to improve native plant stocks

6

Extract Four

You hear part of a talk about science and public opinion.

7 The speaker uses the example of genetics to underline people's

   A   vulnerability in the face of false claims.
   B   willingness to believe a good story.
   C   inability to understand deep concepts.

7

8 What is the speaker doing in this part of the talk?

   A   complaining about our lack of imagination
   B   encouraging us to take science more seriously
   C   questioning our faith in scientific findings

8

Part 2

You will hear a man called Derek Lane giving a talk on the subject of ancient trees. For questions **9–17**, complete the sentences with a word or short phrase.

Ancient trees were once believed to possess

	9

and played an important role in folk tales.

Ancient trees were often used as a venue for both religious and

	10

events in past times.

The oldest tree, known as the creosote bush, has a distinctive

	11

Researchers did not expect to find ancient trees in areas classified as

	12

In recent research, a technique known as

	13

was used to calculate the age of trees.

Recently it has become possible to collect information about

	14

by analysing ancient trees.

Derek explains that it is a mistake to regard

	15

trees as being unhealthy in any way.

The technique known as coppicing was designed to produce a long-term

	16

supply.

Many species of wildlife rely on the process of

	17

in old tree trunks.

Part 3

You will hear a radio discussion on the subject of dictionaries. For questions **18–22**, choose the answer (**A**, **B**, **C** or **D**) which fits best according to what you hear.

18 Elaine says she is under pressure at work as a result of

    A the growth of the market.
    B the quality of the competition.
    C the demand for greater profits.
    D the need to manage resources.

          18

19 Elaine decides to include a word in her dictionaries after checking

    A how it is used in the press.
    B whether it is on the database.
    C what researchers think of it.
    D whether its use is widespread.

          19

20 According to Elaine, in which area of her work has new technology had the greatest impact?

    A the accuracy of the entries
    B the speed of the research
    C the reliability of the data
    D the quality of the language

          20

21 According to Tony, what may influence a dictionary compiler's decision to include a particular term?

    A technical experience
    B reading habits
    C personal interests
    D objective research

          21

22 According to Elaine, what prevents dictionary compilers from inventing words themselves?

    A respect for their colleagues
    B lack of inspiration
    C fear of criticism
    D pride in their work

          22

Part 4

You will hear part of a conversation in which two friends, Maria and Stuart, are discussing Maria's search for a new job. For questions **23–28**, decide whether the opinions are expressed by only one of the speakers, or whether the speakers agree.

Write: **M** for Maria,

S for Stuart,

or **B** for Both, where they agree.

---

23 I find a poor working environment unacceptable.

| | 23 |

24 I expect to have several changes of direction in my career.

| | 24 |

25 Internal promotion does not necessarily depend on good working relationships.

| | 25 |

26 It is important to have the security of a signed contract.

| | 26 |

27 Looking for a new job is an exciting challenge.

| | 27 |

28 What I do for a living is part of the image I present to the world.

| | 28 |

PAPER 5   SPEAKING (19 minutes)

There are two examiners. One (the interlocutor) conducts the test, providing you with the necessary materials and explaining what you have to do. The other examiner (the assessor) will be introduced to you, but then takes no further part in the interaction.

Part 1 (3 minutes)

The interlocutor first asks you and your partner a few questions which focus on information about yourselves and personal opinions.

Part 2 (4 minutes)

In this part of the test you and your partner are asked to talk together. The interlocutor places a set of pictures on the table in front of you. There may be only one picture in the set or as many as seven pictures. This stimulus provides the basis for a discussion. The interlocutor first asks an introductory question which focuses on two of the pictures (or in the case of a single picture, on aspects of the picture). After about a minute, the interlocutor gives you both a decision-making task based on the same set of pictures.

The picture for Part 2 is on page C4 of the colour section.

Part 3 (12 minutes)

You are each given the opportunity to talk for two minutes, to comment after your partner has spoken and to take part in a more general discussion.

The interlocutor gives you a card with a question written on it and asks you to talk about it for two minutes. After you have spoken, your partner is first asked to comment and then the interlocutor asks you both another question related to the topic on the card. This procedure is repeated, so that your partner receives a card and speaks for two minutes, you are given an opportunity to comment and a follow-up question is asked.

Finally, the interlocutor asks some further questions, which leads to a discussion on a general theme related to the subjects already covered in Part 3.

The cards for Part 3 are on pages C5 and C10 of the colour section.

Test 3

PAPER 1   READING (1 hour 30 minutes)

Part 1

For questions **1–18**, read the three texts below and decide which answer (**A**, **B**, **C** or **D**) best fits each gap.

Mark your answers **on the separate answer sheet**.

___

Listing

In Britain the badge of distinction awarded to historic buildings is unheroically called 'listing'. When a building is listed it is **(1)** .... for preservation and it is expected to stand more or less indefinitely – nobody expects it to be demolished, ever. But what is the **(2)** .... expectancy of, **(3)** .... , a nineteenth-century terraced house? A few years ago most people assumed that such houses would eventually wear out and be replaced – and millions were demolished in slum **(4)** ..... . But about 2.5 million of these terraces survive, and in some towns they are being given 'conservation area' **(5)** .... , so don't expect the bulldozers there. The very low rates of demolition and construction in the UK **(6)** .... that the building stock as a whole is ageing, and this has enormous implications for the long-term sustainability of housing.

1 A branded	**B** earmarked	**C** minted	**D** tagged
2 A time	**B** age	**C** strength	**D** life
3 A say	**B** imagine	**C** think	**D** look
4 A removal	**B** riddance	**C** clearance	**D** dispatch
5 A quality	**B** class	**C** rank	**D** status
6 A mean	**B** convey	**C** explain	**D** determine

Shopping in Europe

The first self-service stores opened in America in the 1920s but they didn't catch on in Europe until later, when the French forged ahead with their massive hypermarkets. Britain **(7)** .... behind. Although the first self-service shop and the first supermarket were opened in the early 1940s, it was thought that British housewives did not particularly want efficiency and speed. Surveys showed that while American shoppers complained most about delays in check-out queues, British ones objected to being pushed and **(8)** .... by other customers.

The **(9)** .... of supermarket shopping is impersonality, with no mediating salesman between shopper and goods, only the 'silent persuaders' of packaging and display. However, there is a current **(10)** .... towards 'boutiques', with personal service, within supermarkets – the butcher, the baker, the fishmonger – and small specialist shops and farmers' markets are making a **(11)** .... in Britain. In France, where every **(12)** .... provincial town, ringed by supermarkets, retains its specialist food shops and weekly street market, the traditional co-exists with the new.

7 A dwelled	**B** clung	**C** deferred	**D** lagged
8 A thrust	**B** shoved	**C** heaved	**D** jerked
9 A crux	**B** key	**C** gist	**D** essence
10 A momentum	**B** trend	**C** craze	**D** vogue
11 A comeback	**B** rebound	**C** rally	**D** pick-up
12 A self-regarding	**B** self-appointed	**C** self-respecting	**D** self-conscious

Teeth

Smile at yourself in the mirror. Do you like what you see? If not, cosmetic dentistry could be the answer. 'Dentistry has **(13)** .... a long way since the days of simple fillings and extractions,' says London dental surgeon Dr Phil Stemmer, whose client list at his Teeth For Life clinic **(14)** .... pop stars, actresses and even royalty, although his lips are tightly **(15)** .... on names. 'More and more people are turning to dentistry as a way of improving appearance,' he says. 'Shape, form, colour and alignment all make noticeable differences to a smile, and by creating an improved smile I can dramatically alter a person's whole **(16)** .... of themselves.' Top actress Julia Roberts seems to be universally **(17)** .... as the 'gold standard' in smiles, and, following her lead, one of the first things top models invest in is a perfect set of teeth to improve their chances of becoming cover-girl **(18)** .... .

13 A gone	**B** been	**C** come	**D** done
14 A proclaims	**B** brags	**C** trumpets	**D** boasts
15 A closed	**B** glued	**C** sealed	**D** shut
16 A perception	**B** observation	**C** discernment	**D** consciousness
17 A cheered	**B** hailed	**C** saluted	**D** exalted
18 A stuff	**B** substance	**C** material	**D** matter

Part 2

You are going to read four extracts which are all concerned in some way with advertising and publicity. For questions **19–26**, choose the answer (**A**, **B**, **C** or **D**) which you think fits best according to the text.

Mark your answers **on the separate answer sheet**.

Advertising in the US

A kind of creeping illiteracy invaded advertising in the US in the 1950s, to the dismay of many. By 1958 Ford was advertising that you could 'travel smooth' in a Thunderbird Sunliner and the maker of Ace Combs was urging buyers to 'comb it handsome' – a trend that continues today with 'pantihose that fits you real comfortable' and other linguistic manglings too numerous and dispiriting to dwell on.

We may smile at the advertising ruses of the past but in fact such manipulation still goes on, albeit at a more sophisticated level. The *New York Times Magazine* reported in 1990 how an advertising copywriter had been told to come up with some impressive labels for a putative hand cream. She invented the arresting and healthful-sounding term 'oxygenating moisturizers', and wrote the accompanying text with references to 'tiny bubbles of oxygen that release moisture into your skin'. This done, her work was turned over to the company's research and development department, which was instructed to come up with a product that matched the text.

Truth has seldom been a particularly visible feature of American advertising. And has all this deviousness led to a tightening of the rules concerning what is allowable in advertising? Hardly. In 1986, as William Lutz relates in *Doublespeak*, the insurance company John Hancock launched an ad campaign in which 'real people in real situations' discussed their financial predicaments with remarkable candour. When a journalist asked to speak to these real people, a company spokesman conceded that they were actors and 'in that sense they are not real people'.

line 3 (dismay of many. By 1958 Ford was)

line 10 (manglings too numerous and dispiriting)

line 19 (a putative hand cream. She invented the)

line 39 (with remarkable candour. When a)

19   What is the writer's point about the advertisement for a hand cream?

    A   It existed before the product was created.
    B   It inaccurately described the product.
    C   It caused controversy when it came out.
    D   It made the product sound interesting.

20   Which of these words is used to express disapproval on the part of the writer?

    A   dismay (line 3)
    B   manglings (line 10)
    C   putative (line 19)
    D   candour (line 39)

A New Copywriter

Mr Bredon had been a week with Pym's publicity, and had learnt a number of things. He learned the average number of words that can be crammed into four inches of copy; that the word 'pure' was dangerous, because if lightly used, it laid the client open to prosecution by the Government inspectors, whereas the words 'highest quality', 'finest ingredients', 'packed under the best conditions' had no legal meaning, and were therefore safe; that the most convincing copy was always written with the tongue in the cheek, since a genuine conviction of the commodity's worth produced – for some reason – poverty and flatness of style; that if, by the most far-fetched stretch of ingenuity, an indecent meaning could be read into a headline, that was the meaning that the great British Public would infallibly read into it; that the great aim and object of the studio artist was to crowd the copy out of the advertisement and that, conversely, the copywriter was a designing villain whose ambition was to cram the space with verbiage and leave no room for the sketch; that the layout man, a meek ass between two burdens, spent a miserable life trying to reconcile these opposing parties; and further, that all departments alike united in hatred of the client, who persisted in spoiling good layouts by cluttering them up with coupons, free-gift offers, lists of local agents and realistic portraits of hideous and uninteresting cartons, to the detriment of his own interests and the annoyance of everybody concerned.

21 Mr Bredon learnt that there was tension between artists and copywriters because

    A   they each felt that the other exerted too much influence on the layout man.
    B   no attempt was made to get them to work together.
    C   decisions about the final content of advertisements kept changing.
    D   they each felt that their individual contribution was the most important.

22 Mr Bredon learnt that clients were unpopular because

    A   they directly caused advertisements for their products to be unappealing.
    B   they were conservative in their approach to what advertisements should contain.
    C   they demanded that the content of advertisements should be re-arranged.
    D   they treated the people who produced their advertisements with contempt.

Nick Drake and his record company

Island Records had as much faith in Nick Drake as anyone, but in those antediluvian times before videos, the only way an audience got to see an act whose record they liked was in performance. And playing live was something which Nick was beginning to have a serious problem with. For him, the very idea of 'promoting product' was probably anathema; but it was essential for acts to be seen, not just heard. Nick's reluctance to perform effectively cut off the prime avenue of exposure for any new act, a fact which did not escape his record label. David Sandison explains: 'There was interest from a few people but it was limited. It was "Yeah, that's nice, but so what?" … And that's understandable. There wasn't any profile. There wasn't anything to grab on to. There wasn't even explaining the songs in interviews. There wasn't any gigging so that you could make that live connection.'

In the light of frequent allegations of his record company's indifference, it is interesting that Gabrielle feels strongly that Island could not have been more supportive of her brother. 'Island was not where the problem lay. I read about Nick railing that he wasn't more famous, but in the end, you jolly well have to set about becoming famous. As a young artist of any sort, you have to push. I think he was very lucky – he was also extraordinarily talented – but he found somewhere like Island who were prepared to support him, nurture him, and not mind that he didn't do the publicity.'

23 What does David Sandison say about Nick Drake?

  A   Some people began to lose patience with him.
  B   His image was wrong.
  C   He wasn't a very appealing person.
  D   People didn't have much to say about him.

24 What view is expressed by Nick Drake's sister?

  A   He was much misunderstood.
  B   He wasn't aware of how great his talent was.
  C   He had opportunities that he didn't take.
  D   He never wanted to be popular.

Visual materials for Paper 5

1A

1B

1C

1D

1E

1F

1G

TEST 1

Prompt card 1a

In general, how well are children taught in schools?

- teaching methods
- subjects and skills
- importance of discipline

TEST 2

Prompt card 2a

What responsibilities do individuals have towards other people?

- the family
- friends and colleagues
- the world

TEST 3

Prompt card 3a

What attracts people to living in capital cities?

- opportunities
- ambition
- variety

TEST 4

Prompt card 4a

What use is art to society?

- enjoyment
- education
- decoration

3A

3B

3C

3D

3E

3F

4A

4B

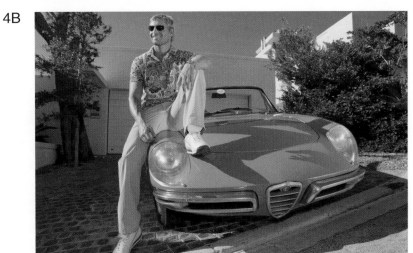

4C

4D

4E

4F

4G

TEST 1

What kind of things cannot be learnt from books?

- sense of responsibility
- experience
- social skills

TEST 2

How easy is it for people to work together?

- personalities
- goals
- technology

TEST 3

Why do some people become the centre of attention?

- character
- talent
- circumstances

TEST 4

Why do people follow fashion in clothes?

- men and women
- identity
- pressures

Advertising agencies and their clients

Advertising agencies have long been viewed by their clients with a mixture of wariness and envy. Fat pay cheques and fast cars remain an enduring image. But things have changed. British advertising agencies are turning to training: not just for their own staff but for their clients as well. Role reversal has become a novel way of educating companies which use advertisements in the advertising agency's darkest arts.

The agency LHS last month staged its first role reversal course. It involved 19 managers from 15 different companies and their task was to plan and create an entire campaign within 48 hours, culminating in a pitch for the £5m advertising business for a fictitious product launch. Participants were divided into groups of five or six. Their first job was to create a brief to advertise a new ice cream bar. Briefs were then swapped and each group became an 'agency'. The agencies' first task was to interpret the brief. 'These were of decidedly mixed quality,' Kevin Duncan of LHS said. 'Clear briefs elicit no questions. Poor briefs generate many – and no answers.' They then had to decide their strategy. They were given market and media data, though some of this was erroneous, 'to illustrate how a good brand manager sifts information in advance'.

The next step was to develop a creative approach and by the end of the first full day the agencies were expected to be in a position to test their ideas with research groups made up of members of the public. Interpreting the results of qualitative research is critical, Mr Duncan said. 'People wilfully interpret research findings to post-rationalise their ideas.'

25 On the LHS agency's course, what did participants have to do?

A design a new product
B try to win a contract
C move from group to group
D negotiate a budget

26 What is said about research groups?

A People in advertising get confused by what they say.
B People in advertising pay too much attention to them.
C People in advertising pretend that they have been proved right by them.
D People in advertising change their strategies as a result of what they say.

Part 3

You are going to read an article about a jazz record. Seven paragraphs have been removed from the extract. Choose from the paragraphs **A–H** the one which fits each gap (**27–33**). There is one extra paragraph which you do not need to use.

Mark your answers **on the separate answer sheet**.

Kind of Blue

As two books celebrate Miles Davis's Kind of Blue, *Martin Gayford salutes a towering achievement.*

What is the greatest jazz album ever made? Perhaps it's an impossible question, but there is a strong candidate in *Kind of Blue*, recorded by the Miles Davis Sextet in the spring of 1959. It is the one jazz album owned by many people who don't really like jazz at all.

27

And for many who do love jazz, this is the one record that they would choose to take with them to a desert island. If he had to select one record to explain what jazz is, producer and arranger Quincy Jones has said, this would be it (he himself plays it every day – 'It's my orange juice').

28

What is so special about *Kind of Blue*? First, it was made by a magnificent band. Apart from Davis himself, *Kind of Blue* features John Coltrane on tenor saxophone, Cannonball Adderley on alto, and Bill Evans on piano – all among the finest performers of that era, and at the height of their powers. And, unlike many all-star recordings, the players were at ease in each other's musical company, as this was a working group (or almost).

29

Everybody was on the most inspired form. That does not happen every day, and is particularly unlikely to happen in the tense and clinical atmosphere of the recording studio. Other jazz performers, for example the saxophonist Sonny Rollins and the trumpeter Roy Eldridge, have spoken of rare days on which some external force seems to take over their instrument, and they can do no wrong.

30

Evans wrote about that spur-of-the-moment freshness in his original notes for the album. Each of the five pieces on the album, he claimed, was recorded in a single take, and the musicians had never seen the music before, as Miles was still working on it hours before the recording sessions. Davis was credited with all the compositions.

31

The key to *Kind of Blue* lies in the enigmatic personality of Davis, who died in 1991. He was an irascible, contrary, foul-mouthed, aggressive man who, it seems, sheltered within an extremely sensitive soul. 'Miles talks rough,' claimed trumpeter Dizzy Gillespie, 'but his music reveals his true character ... Miles is shy. He is super-shy.' As a young man, playing with Charlie Parker, Davis was so paralysed with terror that he sometimes had to be pushed on stage. At that time he seriously considered forsaking music for dentistry.

32

'I think,' he said in 1958, 'that a movement in jazz is beginning, away from a conventional string of chords – a return to an emphasis on melodic rather than harmonic variations. There will be fewer chords, but infinite possibilities as to what to do with them.' 'Classical composers,' he went on, 'some of them have been working that way for years.' Indeed, Davis's feeling for European music – Ravel, Khachaturian, Rachmaninov – colours *Kind of Blue*. He disliked most attempts to blend classical and jazz – so-called 'third stream music'.

33

It is a completely integrated, freely improvised album of unhackneyed, moving music. Davis never sounded better – and in his heart, he knew it.

A Over the years he developed a tough carapace. But in a music characterised by extroversion and ostentatious virtuosity, he developed a style that became ever more muted, subtle, melodic and melancholy.

B Firstly, most of Davis's albums were largely recorded in one take per tune. He seems to have believed that first thoughts were the freshest (the alternative, adopted by Bill Evans and Coltrane on their own recordings, is to do takes by the dozen in a search for perfection). And the other point about *Kind of Blue* is its musical novelty. As revered pianist Chick Corea has put it, 'It's one thing to play a tune or a programme of music, but it's another to practically create a new language of music, which is what *Kind of Blue* did.'

C Now comes another sign of renown. How many jazz recordings are the subject of even one book? This spring, not one but two are being published on the subject of *Kind of Blue*. There is *Kind of Blue: The Making of a Jazz Masterpiece* by Ashley Kahn and, published in the US, *The Making of Kind of Blue: Miles Davis and his Masterpiece*.

D On closer examination, these celebrated facts, which make *Kind of Blue* seem almost supernatural, are only partially true. Two tracks, *So What* and *All Blues*, had been played previously by the band, on the road, which Evans, not having been with them, probably didn't realise. And Evans himself was largely responsible for the two mesmerisingly beautiful slow pieces, *Blue in Green* and *Flamenco Sketches* – a fact that he modestly suppressed at the time, and then seems to have been quietly resentful about.

E But he did it himself on *Sketches of Spain*, and he loved the playing of Bill Evans, which uniquely combined the feeling of classical piano and the freshness of jazz. The partnership of Davis and Evans is at the heart of *Kind of Blue*, and gives it a wonderful unity of mood – romantic, delicate, hushed on the slow pieces, more exuberant elsewhere.

F The contemporary guitarist John Scofield remembers knocking on strangers' doors when he was a student in the 1970s, and asking if he could borrow their copy. The point was, he knew they would have one.

G On *Kind of Blue*, all the principals seem to feel like that. Davis and Evans, I would say, never played better. The result is something close to the philosopher's stone of jazz: formal perfection attained with perfect spontaneity.

H In fact, Evans had actually resigned the previous November – *Kind of Blue* was made on March 2, and April 22, 1959 – and was invited back for the recording (his replacement, Wynton Kelly, appears on one track).

Part 4

You are going to read an extract from a book about the United States. For questions **34–40**, choose the answer (**A**, **B**, **C** or **D**) which you think fits best according to the text.

Mark your answers **on the separate answer sheet**.

Sound and Fury

If I had to instruct a stranger on the contrasts between the United States and Britain, I would start with some televised weather reports from the two countries.

In Britain, the weather is presented in a mild, diffident, terribly-sorry-for-the-inconvenience manner. There's not much variety or excitement. The typical British weatherman appears in front of the camera with his head lowered, shoulders hunched, hands clasped and jacket buttoned. He speaks softly, almost meekly, as if telling a child's bedtime story. He points to curvy isobars that bend into the country from the sea. They all seem to mean the same thing. He might talk positively about 'sun and showers' or 'sunny spells', but usually the day will be 'dull'. In Britain the weather is so lacking in spirit that it is reported apologetically.

In America, on the other hand, the weather is pitched with the verve customarily reserved for a used-car lot. American weathermen report the next day's outlook as if they were trying to sell it to you. There's always a lot to talk about and big things are happening out there. Most prognostications are delivered in a you're-not-going-to-believe-me tone of voice. There are heatwaves in one part of the country and blizzards in another. Hot fronts and cold fronts march across the map. A freeze oozes ominously down from the Canadian wastes, and a tropical storm builds up in the Caribbean. American weather is raucous, and so are American weathermen.

American weather is also intimidating in a manner you hardly ever see in the equable British climate. Americans know their weather and they watch it warily. In my wife's home town in South Carolina, for example, the heat comes early in the year, balmy and lulling at the start of spring. But by the summer high it spreads out across the land like a heavy duvet. You can almost cup the humidity in your hands, and it's impossible to take more than a few steps without breaking into a glistening sweat. There is no relief at night. And when it rains there, it rains apocalyptically. The heat gathers itself up in a darkening sky, and by the afternoon there is a still, humid anticipation that something epic is about to burst. The trees rustle and the land goes quiet until a sudden split of lightning streaks across the black heaven and a cracking slip of thunder makes the clouds rumble. The earth shakes and the rain comes down as if the bottom of the sky had collapsed under its weight. It beats against the land in fat, hammering drops, filling the streets with torrents.

As rainy as it is in Britain, it never rains this way. Here, the sky looks like a grey veil. It often seems about to rain but it takes for ever to get on with it. And when the rain finally comes, it sprays down as if the sky had sprung a couple of small leaks, and you think more of nourishment than calamity.

The American climate can be so quixotic and so destructive that the federal government and the National Weather Service have established a network of 450 radio transmitters across the nation to beam warnings of potential hazards to unwary communities, and commercial radio stations are required to test their civil emergency systems at regular intervals. An American cable television channel offers twenty-four-hour coverage of the weather. The Federal Emergency Management Agency is geared to respond to the natural disasters that regularly afflict the nation, and a president or state governor runs major political risks if he fails to react swiftly enough to a civil calamity.

The moderation of British weather and the volatility of American weather fit naturally with the character of the two countries. The climate in Britain is hardly ever out of **line** sorts. A wind storm or drought are major aberrations. Except for the swings of daylight, it's sometimes difficult to tell one season from another, so subtle are the shifts in pattern.

American weather is the opposite. A meteorological study once concluded that there were two places on earth which could boast the world's worst weather; the Gobi Desert and Amarillo, Texas. For extremes of heat, cold, wind, rain and so forth, it's hard to beat Amarillo. But what is true of Texas is more or less true of the rest of the country as well. In 1995, a heatwave incinerated the Midwest and East Coast with temperatures as high as 43°C reported daily for a week. On average there are 106 complete days of fog in the appropriately named Cape Disappointment, Washington, and in nearby and inappropriately named Paradise 3, 109 cm of snow fell in the winter of 1972. And in the winter of 1993, the wind chill temperature in Devil's Lake, Wisconsin touched −33°C.

Drizzle and sunny spells in Britain. The climate is moderate and restrained, with no extremes of anything, and so the isle is green and providential. Fire and ice in America. The climate is fearsome and doesn't work by half-measures.

34 It is the writer's opinion that British weathermen

    A   are not aware that they are being patronising to viewers.
    B   talk as if they are personally responsible for the weather.
    C   do not feel that weather reports ought to be entertaining.
    D   have little enthusiasm for presenting weather reports on TV.

35 The writer says that US weather reports

    A   are intended to impress viewers.
    B   tend to exaggerate the real situation.
    C   are often rather confusing for viewers.
    D   tend to be entertaining rather than informative.

36 What does the writer seek to illustrate by mentioning the weather in his wife's home town?

    A   the tendency of American people to complain about the weather
    B   how unpleasant he finds certain weather conditions
    C   the unpredictable nature of the weather in certain parts of America
    D   why Americans treat the climate with such respect

37 What does the writer say about rain in Britain?

    A   He looks forward to it.
    B   There is less of it than people think.
    C   It gives no cause for anxiety.
    D   It depresses people living there.

38 The writer mentions the US federal government to illustrate

    A   how important an issue the weather is in America.
    B   past failures to deal efficiently with problems caused by the weather.
    C   how complicated the situation is concerning the weather in America.
    D   the public's annoyance when terrible weather conditions suddenly affect them.

39 What does the writer mean when he says that the climate in Britain is 'hardly ever out of sorts' (lines 68–69)?

    A   that it has a calming influence
    B   that it is virtually unique
    C   that it is mostly very predictable
    D   that people seldom remark on it

40 The writer includes Cape Disappointment in his list of places in the United States because

    A   it is a place that got its name as a result of the weather conditions there.
    B   it has bad weather conditions a great deal of the time.
    C   it has extreme weather conditions that are not typical in America.
    D   it is a place with a bad reputation among Americans on account of its weather.

PAPER 2   WRITING (2 hours)

Part 1

You **must** answer this question. Write your answer in **300–350** words in an appropriate style.

1 The following comments were made during a radio discussion by young people talking about different attitudes to work. Listeners to the discussion were invited to send in their views to the programme editor. You decide to write a letter responding to the points raised and giving your own opinions.

> I want to earn lots of money – that's all I care about.

> I want a job that leaves me with plenty of free time.

> What matters most to me is job satisfaction. I only want to do a job that I really enjoy.

Write your **letter**. Do not write any addresses.

Part 2

Write an answer to **one** of the questions **2–5** in this part. Write your answer in **300–350** words in an appropriate style.

2   A film magazine is running a series on international cinema. It has invited readers to send in reviews of films set in their own country. You decide to send in a review of such a film considering how effectively the film illustrates particular aspects of life and attitudes in your country.
     Write your **review**.

3   You work for your town council. Your manager has asked you to write a report on a shopping centre which has recently opened in your area. Your report should include consideration of the design and atmosphere of the centre, transport provision and the influence that the centre appears to be having on people's shopping habits.
     Write your **report**.

4   You have read an article in an English language newspaper which states that 'the wheel is our best invention'. The newspaper has invited readers to contribute their own articles suggesting one or two other inventions or discoveries which are as significant as the wheel. You decide to write an article, briefly describing at least one invention or discovery, and explaining its significance to the development of civilisation.
     Write your **article**.

5   Based on your reading of **one** of these books, write on **one** of the following:

   (a)   Chinua Achebe: *Things Fall Apart*
        An international magazine has published a list called *The World's 100 Best Books*, and asked readers to comment on the titles included. *Things Fall Apart* was on the list. You decide to write a letter to the magazine explaining why you think themes such as justice, love and duty appeal to a worldwide audience. You should refer to specific episodes in the novel which support your views.
        Write your **letter**. Do not write any addresses.

   (b)   Ann Patchett: *Bel Canto*
        Your tutor has given you this quotation as the starting point for an essay on *Bel Canto*:
        'During their imprisonment some of the hostages gain a freedom which they never had in their ordinary lives.' Write an essay for your tutor in which you explain in what ways any **two** of the hostages are affected by their imprisonment and the extent to which the quotation applies to those two characters.
        Write your **essay**.

   (c)   J.B. Priestley: *An Inspector Calls*
        A literary magazine is planning a series of articles on the significance of the social settings of plays and novels. You decide to submit an article on *An Inspector Calls*. You should describe Mr Birling's views on society and examine to what extent Sheila and Eric are influenced by their family background in the way they respond to the evening's events.
        Write your **article**.

PAPER 3   USE OF ENGLISH (1 hour 30 minutes)

Part 1

For questions **1–15**, read the text below and think of the word which best fits each space. Use only **one** word in each space. There is an example at the beginning **(0)**.

Write your answers in CAPITAL LETTERS **on the separate answer sheet**.

Example: `0` | `O` | `N` | | | | | | | | | | | | | | | | | | | | |

The Psychology of Selling

The psychology of retailing has come to rely **(0)**........ON...... highly sophisticated techniques. Over and **(1)**............ the design of the shops and the packaging of the merchandise, clever positioning of goods also ensures that the natural flow of people takes them to **(2)**............ and every section in a shop. Customers are led gently, but at the **(3)**............ time with deadly accuracy, towards the merchandise in such a way **(4)**............ to maximise sales.

Manufacturers compete for the right to **(5)**............ their products displayed at the **(6)**............ effective level. In supermarkets, there is a crucial section in the tiers of vertical shelving somewhere **(7)**............ waist height and eye level, where we are most likely to **(8)**............ note of a brand. In the old days, when we went into a shop, we made our **(9)**............ up to the counter, behind **(10)**............ would be the shopkeeper and virtually all of the merchandise, and were served with what we wanted. Those days are **(11)**............ and truly over.

Today, we are used to serving **(12)**............ in supermarkets; products are laid before us as enticingly as **(13)**............ , and impulse purchases are encouraged as a major part of the exercise. As a **(14)**............ of this, we, as shoppers, have to keep our wits **(15)**............ us to resist the retailers' ploys.

Part 2

For questions **16–25**, read the text below. Use the word given in capitals at the end of some of the lines to form a word that fits in the space in the same line. There is an example at the beginning **(0)**.

Write your answers in CAPITAL LETTERS **on the separate answer sheet**.

Example:

| 0 | D | I | S | A | G | R | E | E | | | | | | | | | |

In Good Voice

There is little to **(0)**..DISAGREE.. about in the notion that a good voice, whether   **AGREE**

in opera or rock music, is one which moves its audience and brings a sense

of release and fulfilment to the singer. But contemporary pop and rock music

have come about due to **(16)**............ advances in technology. Here, the   **SUBSTANCE**

impact of the microphone should not be **(17)**............ , as it has   **ESTIMATE**

(18)............ the magnification of quiet, intimate sounds. This, in turn, allows   **ABLE**

the singer to experiment with the **(19)**............ on mood rather than on strict   **EMPHATIC**

(20)............ to proper breathing and voice control.   **ADHERE**

Donna Soto-Morettin, a rock and jazz vocal trainer, feels that **(21)**............   **ANATOMY**

reasons may account for the raspy sound produced by certain rock singers. Her

(22)............ is that swollen vocal chords, which do not close properly, may   **SUSPECT**

allow singers to produce deeper notes. She does not, however, regard this as

detracting **(23)**............ from the value of the sound produced. Singing, she   **NOTICE**

maintains, has an almost **(24)**............ quality and so our response to it has   **SEDUCE**

more **(25)**............ than its technical qualities.   **SIGNIFY**

Part 3

For questions **26–31**, think of **one** word only which can be used appropriately in all three sentences. Here is an example **(0)**.

Example:

0 Some of the tourists are hoping to get compensation for the poor state of the hotel, and I think they have a very .... case.

There's no point in trying to wade across the river, the current is far too ....

If you're asking me which of the candidates should get the job, I'm afraid I don't have any .... views either way.

| 0 | S | T | R | O | N | G | | | | | | | | | | | |

Write **only** the missing word in CAPITAL LETTERS **on the separate answer sheet**.

---

26 There's a .... in the text at this point, so the meaning is far from clear.

After a period of unemployment, the actor had a lucky .... and got the starring role in a big musical.

During the meeting, there was a .... in the proceedings while the votes were counted.

27 It took the children some time to .... down after the excitement of seeing their school win the football match.

Ivana has decided that she definitely wants to .... in America.

Stefan says the time has come to .... this matter once and for all.

28 Children's imaginations are often .... by trips out of school.

Mr Henderson closed the door, told me to sit down and said the words which I had been dreading, 'You're .... !'

The race began when the starter's gun was ....

29   The travel agent says we should .... an extra hour for our journey in case of delays.

The owners of the estate do not .... fishing in the lake.

How much pocket money does Boris .... his children each week?

30   If you can .... yourself away from the television for a moment, I'll show you the new CD I've bought.

Wendy entered the tutorial expecting the professor to .... her essay to pieces.

Tennis players are apt to .... ligaments and muscles if they don't train regularly enough.

31   The newspaper reporter was urged to .... the story with sensitivity.

Customers are requested not to .... the goods on display.

The manager couldn't .... the pressure and was forced to resign.

Part 4

For questions **32–39**, complete the second sentence so that it has a similar meaning to the first sentence, using the word given. **Do not change the word given**. You must use between **three** and **eight** words, including the word given.

Here is an example **(0)**.

Example:

0 Do you mind if I watch you while you paint?

objection

Do you .... you while you paint?

0	*have any objection to my watching*

Write **only** the missing words **on the separate answer sheet**.

---

32 Everyone was surprised when the government changed its policy.

took

The government's .... surprise.

33 Celia finally managed to buy her own house after years of saving.

did

Only .... to buy her own house.

34 Nobody could have predicted how quickly the rumour would spread.

speed

The .... could not have been predicted.

35 The sales director told his staff nothing about the new marketing post.

dark

The sales director .... about the new marketing post.

36   Mrs Thomas seems to find the way her daughter behaves more a source of amusement than embarrassment.

   being

   Far .... behaviour, Mrs Thomas seems to be amused by it.

37   The head teacher is well known for his reliability and dedication.

   reputed

   The head teacher .... person.

38   Without access to the statistics, I won't be able to complete the report.

   hold

   Unless I .... the statistics, I won't be able to complete the report.

39   The athletes trained hard because they wanted to make the Olympic team.

   hope

   The athletes trained hard .... the Olympic team.

Part 5

For questions **40–44**, read the following texts on working at home. For questions **40–43**, answer with a word or short phrase. You do not need to write complete sentences. For question **44**, write a summary according to the instructions given.

Write your answers to questions **40–44 on the separate answer sheet**.

According to a recent survey, working from home is an idea whose time has come. Apparently, we are all queuing up not to get the bus, but to carry our favourite coffee mug upstairs and cosy up with the laptop. The overwhelming reason given by those questioned was that they could be much, much more efficient if they worked from home. I can see the obvious advantages but, believe me, working from home is not just inefficient, it is impossible.

You may have a dedicated study in which you can barricade yourself against the general mayhem that is family life, but many people do not. The other awkward truth about home-working is that if, like me, you suffer from the least defect of motivation, you are placing yourself in the   **line 11** grip of mental agony. First there are the household chores you really should do, and then there's that fascinating radio programme …

When I gave up and found a cheap office–share with other self-employees my life improved a hundredfold. I discovered that a distinct break between work and home was crucial for psychological health. When I was at work, I could focus on my task; once I was at home, I could devote myself to the domestic routine.

I realised also that there is something profoundly depressing about working at home. It's as if you haven't got a proper job. Most of us gain self-esteem from our identity as a working person, but there can be no such benefit if the work takes place in social isolation.

40   What verb does the writer use to stress the conflict between work and domesticity?

....

41   Explain in your own words what the phrase 'the least defect of motivation' means in this context. (line 11)

....

Behind the fanfare surrounding a new report on work–life balance lies a truth about the contradictions we all face in juggling home and the workplace. One of the reasons why balancing work and 'life' is so difficult is that work, for many of us, is so appealing.

Work is a gateway to a social network, to friends, to a community. In a world of increased individualism and globalisation, many of us are seeking a sense of belonging somewhere or to someone. On a personal level, the search for belonging takes people to internet chat rooms and clubs, to coffee shops — and to work. Work seems to offer a ready-made community. Psychologically speaking, it satisfies our basic instinct to relate to other individuals, and to society. Gossip sessions at the coffee machine, lazy conversations about holiday plans in the canteen — these all add a social, communitarian dimension to work. Moments of shared meanings remind employees that they belong to a team, a company, something bigger than themselves — thus the workplace fulfils a fundamental human need.   **line 14**

Generally, people are happy both at home and at work. Indeed, work for the majority is quite clearly not the soul-destroying prison it is sometimes perceived to be. There are, of course, those for whom work might be seen as providing an escape, a safe place away from unhappy homes; a distraction from disappointing private lives. However, there are problems where the workplace culture involves very long hours, and people will always need to strike the right balance between work and home.

42   What phrase used earlier in paragraph 2 is echoed by 'a fundamental human need'? (line 14)

    ....

43   What phrase in the final paragraph suggests that some people may find work distinctly unappealing?

    ....

44   In a paragraph of **50–70** words, summarise **in your own words as far as possible** the benefits of going out to work, as described in **both** texts. Write your summary **on the separate answer sheet**.

PAPER 4   LISTENING (40 minutes approximately)

Part 1

You will hear four different extracts. For questions **1–8**, choose the answer (**A**, **B** or **C**) which fits best according to what you hear. There are two questions for each extract.

> **Extract One**

You hear a scientist talking about two spacecraft carrying what he calls a Golden Disc – a type of CD containing information about our civilisation.

1 It was felt that music should be included on the Golden Disc because

   A other life forms would find it beautiful even if it was incomprehensible.
   B other life forms might get an idea of what it is to be human.
   C human languages might not be comprehensible to other life forms.

           1

2 The main reason for the launch of the two spacecraft was to

   A alert other civilisations to our presence.
   B carry the Golden Disc into space.
   C find out more information about space.

           2

> **Extract Two**

In a public lecture, you hear a professor of philosophy talking about a research paper he has just published.

3 In his paper, the professor has attempted to

   A use real-life experiences to disprove a theory.
   B create a fictional world to illustrate his views.
   C find real-world evidence to support his ideas.

           3

4 What is the professor doing when he speaks?

   A justifying the amendments he has made
   B apologising for certain omissions he has made
   C excusing the research methods he used

           4

Extract Three

You hear a woman, Lucy, talking to her friend, John, about his job as a TV journalist.

5 Lucy believes that the use of new technology has resulted in journalists being

    A   less discerning in their choice of material.
    B   able to record more news events.
    C   controlled by new technology.

	5

6 What criterion does John use to decide which events to film?

    A   experience
    B   instinct
    C   visual impact

	6

Extract Four

You hear a film director talking about editing a film for which he also wrote the screenplay.

7 What is he doing when he speaks?

    A   describing his solution to a problem
    B   setting himself targets and objectives
    C   evaluating different approaches to editing

	7

8 He uses the image of renovating a house in order to

    A   justify cuts to the film's length.
    B   explain the process of film editing.
    C   criticise the chaos in the editing studio.

	8

Part 2

You will hear a woman called Gill Firth talking about how she builds houses and other buildings out of straw. For questions **9–17**, complete the sentences with a word or short phrase.

Gill's latest project involves extending a

[   ] **9** at a farm in Scotland.

Gill says that the extension will be [   ] **10** in shape.

Gill says that constructing straw walls is quite similar to building with

[   ] **11**

Gill chooses to use

[   ] **12** pins to fix most of the straw bales together.

Gill explains that she has already installed both [   ] **13**

and electrical wiring in her new building.

Because of the natural qualities of straw, there is no need to

[   ] **14** the walls.

Gill explains that government regulations require her to fit

[   ] **15** in the building.

Gill is currently looking for the investment she needs to build a complete

[   ] **16** out of straw.

Gill feels that communities working in

[   ] **17** would find straw an ideal building material.

Part 3

You will hear an interview with a woman called Alice Cowper who went in search of a rare animal called the king cheetah. For questions **18–22**, choose the answer (**A**, **B**, **C** or **D**) which fits best according to what you hear.

18   What makes the king cheetah different from other cheetahs?

    A   the length of its tail
    B   the pattern on its coat
    C   the width of its stripes
    D   the colour of its spots

        18

19   What did Alice find surprising about her discovery in Botswana?

    A   the number of animals she found
    B   how long it took to find anything
    C   the area where it happened
    D   how hard it was to identify the animal

        19

20   Alice believes that the king cheetah has undergone mutation in order to

    A   protect itself against a new enemy.
    B   prevent the species dying out.
    C   hunt more effectively.
    D   live in different surroundings.

        20

21   Alice explains that the pattern on the king cheetah's coat is

    A   perfectly symmetrical.
    B   frightening to predators.
    C   difficult to describe.
    D   deceptive at first sight.

        21

22   The person who made the comment about the camera people felt that

    A   we should only trust what we see on films.
    B   there is nothing new to find in the world.
    C   adventurers should record their findings.
    D   it is best to look at nature on television.

        22

Part 4

You will hear part of a radio programme in which two people, Jim and Sue, are discussing physical exercise. For questions **23–28**, decide whether the opinions are expressed by only one of the speakers, or whether the speakers agree.

Write: **J** for Jim,
  S for Sue,
or **B** for Both, where they agree.

---

23 The current increase in the number of fitness centres must indicate an improvement in people's health. | 23 |

24 Many people believe whatever the media tell them about health issues. | 24 |

25 Many people fail to exercise regularly because they have too many other commitments. | 25 |

26 It's easier to maintain a fitness programme when you exercise with a group of friends. | 26 |

27 Group exercise sessions during working hours benefit employees. | 27 |

28 The provision of company sports facilities is a good way to encourage fitness. | 28 |

PAPER 5   SPEAKING (19 minutes)

There are two examiners. One (the interlocutor) conducts the test, providing you with the necessary materials and explaining what you have to do. The other examiner (the assessor) will be introduced to you, but then takes no further part in the interaction.

Part 1 (3 minutes)

The interlocutor first asks you and your partner a few questions which focus on information about yourselves and personal opinions.

Part 2 (4 minutes)

In this part of the test you and your partner are asked to talk together. The interlocutor places a set of pictures on the table in front of you. There may be only one picture in the set or as many as seven pictures. This stimulus provides the basis for a discussion. The interlocutor first asks an introductory question which focuses on two of the pictures (or in the case of a single picture, on aspects of the picture). After about a minute, the interlocutor gives you both a decision-making task based on the same set of pictures.

   The pictures for Part 2 are on pages C6–C7 of the colour section.

Part 3 (12 minutes)

You are each given the opportunity to talk for two minutes, to comment after your partner has spoken and to take part in a more general discussion.

   The interlocutor gives you a card with a question written on it and asks you to talk about it for two minutes. After you have spoken, your partner is first asked to comment and then the interlocutor asks you both another question related to the topic on the card. This procedure is repeated, so that your partner receives a card and speaks for two minutes, you are given an opportunity to comment and a follow-up question is asked.

   Finally, the interlocutor asks some further questions, which leads to a discussion on a general theme related to the subjects already covered in Part 3.

   The cards for Part 3 are on pages C5 and C10 of the colour section.

Test 4

PAPER 1   READING (1 hour 30 minutes)

Part 1

For questions **1–18**, read the three texts below and decide which answer (**A**, **B**, **C** or **D**) best fits each gap.

Mark your answers **on the separate answer sheet**.

Flight to Phoenix

I was booked on an early flight so I **(1)** .... no time in getting showered and dressed, and **(2)** .... for the airport. It was only when I felt the aircraft leave the runway, and saw Manhattan **(3)** .... into the distance beneath and behind me, that I finally began to relax.

Even at nine o'clock in the morning Phoenix was hot. It was a physical shock to walk out of the cool, dark terminal into the bright reflection of the sunlight. Locals ambled slowly past in short-sleeved shirts and sunglasses. In less than a minute I was sweating in my suit as I carried my bags over to the large sign which read 'Bloomfield Weiss High Yield Bond Conference'.

They had **(4)** .... on white stretch limousines to take the conference participants to the hotel. Within seconds, I was back in air-conditioned quiet again. I supposed that it was **(5)** .... possible to spend all of your life in Phoenix at 18° centigrade, with only brief **(6)** .... of extra heat as you transferred from air-conditioned house to air-conditioned car to air-conditioned office.

1	**A** used	**B** lost	**C** left	**D** made
2	**A** headed	**B** pressed	**C** proceeded	**D** set
3	**A** abating	**B** withdrawing	**C** receding	**D** reversing
4	**A** laid	**B** catered	**C** sorted	**D** furnished
5	**A** purely	**B** perfectly	**C** starkly	**D** solidly
6	**A** gales	**B** torrents	**C** fits	**D** bursts

Keas – not just pretty parrots

Few birds are as **(7)** .... curious as keas. New research shows how these New Zealand parrots channel that curiosity for maximum benefit: they **(8)** .... up tips by watching each other. Keas are notorious for investigating and, in the **(9)** .... , often destroying everything from rubbish bins to windscreen wipers. Ludwig Huber and colleagues from the University of Vienna have found that in keas, which live in family flocks, social learning affects patterns of curiosity. In their experiments, the keas' task was to open a steel box with a complex locking mechanism. Two birds were gradually trained as 'models' and then they **(10)** .... the task again under the watchful gaze of keas who were new to the job. **(11)** .... enough, birds who had watched a demonstration had a much higher success **(12)** .... than keas who had never watched one.

7 **A** insatiably	**B** hungrily	**C** thirstily	**D** unmanageably
8 **A** take	**B** lift	**C** pick	**D** pull
9 **A** procedure	**B** process ✓	**C** measure	**D** technique
10 **A** enacted	**B** staged	**C** performed	**D** presented
11 **A** Certain	**B** Sure	**C** True	**D** Fair
12 **A** proportion	**B** percentage	**C** occurrence	**D** rate

Bureaucracy

Given that bureaucracy is held in such ill **(13)** .... today, it is hard to remember that it was once considered a great organisational innovation. By organising the **(14)** .... of labour, by making management and decision-making a profession, and by providing an order and a set of rules that allowed many different kinds of specialists to work in coordination toward a common **(15)** ...., bureaucracy greatly extended the breadth and depth of intelligence that organisations could achieve. Begun as a system of organising government activities, it has **(16)** .... to big business and large organisations of all kinds.

Max Weber, who **(17)** .... the systematic study of bureaucracy as its role in western society began to explode in the late nineteenth century, saw bureaucracy as both the most efficient possible system, and a threat to the basic liberties he **(18)** .... dear, thus foreshadowing the sentiments which bureaucracy frequently evokes today.

13 **A** notoriety	**B** knowledge	**C** repute	**D** name
14 **A** division	**B** distinction	**C** detachment	**D** divergence
15 **A** end	**B** finish	**C** culmination	**D** termination
16 **A** carried	**B** spread	**C** transmitted	**D** caught
17 **A** opened	**B** sprang	**C** launched	**D** fired
18 **A** loved	**B** felt	**C** knew	**D** held

You are going to read four extracts which are all concerned in some way with music and musicians. For questions **19–26**, choose the answer (**A**, **B**, **C** or **D**) which you think fits best according to the text.

Mark your answers **on the separate answer sheet**.

Rock Journalism

Back in the 1960s, when rock music journalism was in its infancy, great pieces of writing stood head and shoulders above the rest. These days it has become so commonplace, so everyday, that true opinion, true experience and true style have become difficult to find. Reading a lot of rock writing nowadays you start to wonder why the people involved picked up a pen in the first place.

These days the rock'n'roll lifestyle has become a cliché. In fact the myth of Beatledom (a lifetime squeezed into ten short years) is now so well-known, so much a part of modern history, that it can be emulated (at least in theory) by fledgling rock stars from places as far apart as St Petersburg and Auckland. Back in the days when Rod Stewart wanted to be a rock star he was more or less escaping the drudgery of the production line; these days his job comes with a pension plan. It's not surprising that rock journalism has become a cliché too.

19 The writer says that, compared with the 1960s, rock journalism today

    A annoys many readers.
    B confuses many readers.
    C is seldom critical.
    D is mostly unremarkable.

20 The writer uses Rod Stewart as an example of a rock star

    A who has remained popular for a long time.
    B whose motives for becoming one are no longer common.
    C who is typical of many rock stars today.
    D about whom the same kind of things are always written.

Frank Sinatra's press agent

A few days later Nick Sevano brought a new press agent, George Evans, to the show. 'I was bringing George Evans down the aisle to get closer to the stage,' recalled Nick Sevano. 'A girl stood up and threw a rose at Frank and the girl next to her moaned a little. That's all George needed to see. A couple of days later he created an absolute pandemonium for Frank.' After seeing Frank sing at the Paramount, the astute press agent worked with dervishlike energy to turn the sparks of a tossed rose and a moaning teenager into a conflagration of screaming hysterical women.

He hired twelve long-haired, round-faced little girls in bobby socks and paid them five dollars apiece to jump and scream and yell 'Oh, Frankie. Oh, Frankie' when Frank started to sing one of his slow, soft ballads. He drilled them in the basement of the Paramount, directing them to holler when Frank bent and dipped certain notes. 'They shouldn't only yell and squeal, they should fall apart,' Evans said. Two of the girls were coached to fall in a dead faint in the aisle while the others were told to moan in unison as loudly as they could.

To pack the theater to capacity, Evans distributed free tickets to hundreds of youngsters on school vacation. He told a few select columnists that a new young singer was appearing at the Paramount. He said Frank was going to be bigger than any other singer because he made women fall on the floor. Photographers were alerted, and the next day's newspapers showed pictures of young girls being carried out 'in a swoon' after seeing Frank Sinatra. Twelve were hired but thirty fainted.

21 Evans considered it essential that the girls he paid should

A appear to lose control of their emotions completely.
B be genuinely enthusiastic about Sinatra's singing.
C react hysterically throughout Sinatra's performance.
D remain quiet at certain points in the performance.

20 From the text as a whole, we learn that George Evans was

A unpredictable.
B calm.
C shrewd.
D unpleasant.

Book Review

Mozart's letters: edited and translated by Robert Spaethling

Like many 18th and 19th century composers, Wolfgang Amadé Mozart spent a large part of his life on the road. During this time, he impulsively poured his unexpurgated thoughts into copious   line 3
letters home. These are of crucial biographical importance, but their translation is problematic. Mozart had no formal education and wrote in a mixture of German, French and Italian. His grammar and spelling were unruly and his literary efforts idiosyncratic in the   line 7
highest degree. Although the words themselves are easily decoded with the help of bilingual dictionaries, the real problem lies in the tone and, as Robert Spaethling observes, previous translators have ducked this. He points to the inappropriateness of reading the letters in impeccable grammar, and aims rather to preserve the natural flow and flavour of Mozart's original style.   line 13

Spaethling clearly loves words, and linguistic nuance, as much as Mozart did himself. And when the linguistic games are at their most complex, he democratically prints the original alongside the translation so that we can quarrel and do better. The beauty of this work is that now we can see how – casually and seemingly without trying – Mozart parodies the epistolary modes of the day. And it's   line 19
possible to see a connection between this freewheeling brilliance with words and his prodigious musical abilities.

23 Which phrase from the text confirms the idea that Mozart intended his letters to be amusing?

A impulsively poured (line 3)
B idiosyncratic in the highest degree (line 7)
C natural flow and flavour (line 13)
D parodies the epistolary modes (line 19)

24 Which of the following best summarises the reviewer's opinion of the new translation?

A It reveals previously neglected facts about Mozart.
B It throws further light on Mozart's genius.
C It allows a reinterpretation of Mozart's music.
D It underlines the need for further research about Mozart.

HOTSHOTS II
The Beta Band

The Beta Band's forte, aside from occasionally making remarkable music, lies in not liking things. At least so you might think from reading interviews with them, for given half a chance the quartet tends to betray an almost pathological desire to complain: about the rubbish state of pop music today, for instance, or the groups they reckon have ripped them off, or the perfidious behaviour of their record company.

This yen for negation reached its logical conclusion in 1999 when they denounced their own debut album as a meretricious piece of work, the worst that would be released all year. Why? The record company didn't give them enough money, they claimed. Nonsense, came the retort, it was the group's demands that were too extravagant – such as wanting to make a double LP with each of the four sides recorded in a different continent.

Whatever the truth of the matter, the result was that the band punctured much of the excitement they had generated earlier in their career. At their best, they're a quixotically imaginative pop group – with an ability to combine styles creatively – but when it doesn't gel, as on that first album, you get self-indulgence and a frustrating sense of wasted promise.

25 The writer implies that the members of the band have a tendency to be

A unfairly critical of those they work with.
B oversensitive in the face of criticism.
C justifiably critical of other performers.
D over-inclined to criticise each other.

26 In the writer's view, the band's first album was a disappointment because

A it was inadequately funded.
B they failed to promote it effectively.
C it was over-ambitious musically.
D their full potential was not realised.

Part 3

You are going to read an extract from a magazine article. Seven paragraphs have been removed from the extract. Choose from the paragraphs **A–H** the one which fits each gap (**27–33**). There is one extra paragraph which you do not need to use.

Mark your answers **on the separate answer sheet**.

Blind to change

How much of the world around you do you really see? You only take in tiny pieces of information at a time and that can have unnerving consequences, says Laura Spinney.

Imagine you're walking across a college campus when an unknown man asks you for directions. While you're talking, two men pass between you carrying a door. After an irritating minute of interruption you carry on describing the route. When you've finished you are informed that you've just taken part in a psychology experiment, and asked if you noticed any changes after the two men passed with the door. 'No,' you reply uneasily. The unknown man then explains that the man who approached you initially walked off behind the door, leaving this man in his place. You are stunned; the two men are dressed differently and have different voices and haircuts.

| 27 | |

Rather than logging every detail of the visual scene, we are actually highly selective about what we take in. Our impression of seeing everything is just that – an impression. In fact we extract a few details and rely on memory, or perhaps even our imagination, for the rest.

| 28 | |

Yet in 1991, the controversial claim was made that our brains hold only a few salient details about the world – and that this is the reason we are able to function at all. We don't store elaborate pictures in short-term memory, because it isn't necessary and would take up valuable computing power.

| 29 | |

Just a year later, at a conference on perception in Vancouver, it was reported that people shown computer-generated pictures of natural scenes were blind to changes that were made during an eye movement. In a typical laboratory demonstration of this you might be shown a picture on a computer screen of, say, a couple dining on a terrace.

| 30 | |

It's an unnerving experience. But to some extent, such 'change blindness' is artificial because the change is masked in some way. In real life, there tends to be a visible movement that signals the change. But not always. For instance, we have all had the experience of not noticing a traffic signal change because we had briefly looked away.

| 31 | |

For instance, an experiment was done at Harvard in which people were shown a videotape of a basketball game and asked to count the passes made by one or other team. After about 45 seconds a man dressed in a gorilla suit walked slowly across the scene, passing between the players. Although he was visible for five seconds, an amazing 40 per cent of the viewers failed to notice him.

| 32 | |

Such lapses raise important questions about vision. For instance, how can we reconcile these gross lapses with our subjective experience of having continuous access to a rich visual scene? One researcher has actually shown that imagining a scene activates parts of the visual cortex in the same way as seeing it. He says that this supports the idea that we take in just what information we consider important at the time, and fill in the gaps where the details are less important. The illusion that we see 'everything' is partly a result of filling in the gaps using memory. Such memories can be created based on beliefs and expectations.

33

This particular idea has not been generally accepted. Yet most researchers in the field do agree that of all the myriad visual details of any scene that we could record, we take only what is relevant to us at the time. This leads us to the uncomfortable realisation that, for all our subjective experience of a rich visual world, it may, in fact, be impossible to tell what is real and what is imagined.

A Now imagine that the task absorbing their attention had been driving a car, and the distraction had been a pedestrian crossing their path. According to some estimates, nearly half of all motor-vehicle accidents in the US can be attributed to driver error, including momentary loss of attention. It is more than just academic interest that has made both forms of cognitive error hot research topics.

B The image would disappear, to be replaced for a fraction of a second by a blank screen, before reappearing significantly altered – by the raising of a railing in the background, perhaps. Many people search the screen for up to a minute before they see the change. A few never spot it.

C In contrast, other researchers argue that we can get the impression of visual richness without holding any of that richness in our heads. For instance, the 'grand illusion' theory argues that we hold no picture of the visual world in our brains at all. Instead, we refer back to the external visual world as different aspects become important. The illusion arises from the fact that as soon as you ask yourself 'am I seeing this or that?' you turn your attention to it and see it.

D It sounds impossible, but when this test was carried out, a full 50 per cent of those who took part failed to notice the substitution. The subjects had succumbed to what is called change blindness. Taken with a glut of recent experimental results, this phenomenon suggests we see far less than we think we do.

E The relationships between attention, awareness and vision have yet to be clarified. Because we have a less than complete picture of the world at any one time, there is the potential for distortion and error. How that complete picture could be objectively established is controversial, but there is one obvious way forward.

F This flies in the face of what vision researchers have long believed: that seeing really means making pictures in the brain. According to this theory, by building detailed internal representations of the world, and comparing them over time, we would be able to pick out anything that changed.

G And there's a related phenomenon called inattentional blindness, that doesn't need any experimental visual trick at all: if you are not paying attention to some feature of a scene, you won't see it.

H Rather, we log what has changed and assume the rest has stayed the same. Of course, this is bound to mean that we miss a few details. Experimenters had already shown that we may ignore items in the visual field if they appear not to be significant – a repeated word or line on a page of text for instance. But nobody realised quite how little we really do 'see'.

Part 4

You are going to read a magazine article. For questions **34–40**, choose the answer (**A**, **B**, **C** or **D**) which you think fits best according to the text.

Mark your answers **on the separate answer sheet**.

Getting a life – the state of biography today

During a decade in which the British publishing industry was finally obliged to make watchful friends with business, biography has line-managed the cultural transition beautifully. The best biographies still brim with scholarship but they also sell in their thousands. Readers – ordinary ones with birthday presents to get, book vouchers to spend and rainy holidays to fill – love buying books about the life and times of their favourite people. Every year before Christmas, a lorry load of brick-thick biographies appears on the suggestion table in bookshops.

That biography has done so well is thanks to fiction's vacation of middle-ground, that place where authorial and readerly desire just about match. Novels in the last ten years, unable to claim the attention of the common reader, have dispersed across several registers, with the high ground still occupied by those literary novels which continue to play with post-modern concerns about the narrator's impotence, the narrator's fibs and the hero's failure to actually exist.

Biography, by contrast, has until recently shown no such unsettling humility. At its heart lies the biological plot, the birth-to-death arc with triumphs and children, perhaps a middle-aged slump or late-flowering dotted along the way. Pages of footnotes peg this central story, this actual life, into a solid, teeming context. Here was a man or woman who wrote letters, had friends, ate breakfast and smelt a certain way. The process of being written about rematerialises the subject on the page. Writing a life becomes a way of reaffirming that life itself endures.

Until now, that is. Recently biography has started to display all the quivering self-scrutiny which changed the face of fiction twenty years ago. Exhaustion now characterises the genre. All the great lives have been done. But there are ways of proceeding. Ian Hamilton was the pioneer who failed to find J.D. Salinger. Five years later, Janet Malcolm's study of Sylvia Plath, *The Silent Woman*, brilliantly exposed the way in which academics and biographers stalk and hunt one another around the globe in a bid to possess and devour their subject.

The latest in this tradition of books about writing – or not writing – biography is Geoff Dyer's *Out of Sheer Rage*, in which he plots his failure to get started on a study of D.H. Lawrence. Dyer describes every delaying trick familiar to biographers: lugging heavy editions of letters on holiday and then not bothering to unpack; having a motorcycle accident (an extreme prevarication, but preferable to staring at a blank screen); and finally forcing himself to re-read the subject's novels without any pleasure. 'Footstepping' is the new word to describe this approach; 'lifewriting' has become the favoured term on university courses. In the wrong hands, it can become 'so-whatish'. Writers less accomplished than Dyer, Hamilton or Malcolm could be accused of annexing some of their subjects' clout to get mediocre work into print.

The second approach is to write a partial biography, to take a moment or a strand in the subject's life and follow it through without any claims for completeness. This year Ian Hamilton entered the biographical arena again with a slim, sharp examination of why Matthew Arnold stopped writing good poetry once he took up his job as a school inspector. Earlier, Lyndall Gordon's *A Private Life of Henry James* tracked the great man through his odd relationship with two of his female muses. Far from claiming to displace Leon Edel's 'definitive' biography of James, Gordon's book hovered over it, reconfiguring the material into a new and crisper pattern.

The final tack is to move away from a single life altogether, and look at the places where it encounters other events. Dava Sobel's best-selling *Longitude* puts a cultural puzzle at the heart of her story and reads human lives against it. Sebastian Jünger's *The Perfect Storm*, meanwhile, makes the weather its subject, placing the seamen who encounter it into second place. No longer able to demonstrate a human life shaping its destiny, biographers have been obliged to subordinate their subjects to an increasingly detailed context.

Biography will survive its jitters, but it will emerge looking and sounding different. Instead of the huge door-stops of the early 1990s, which claimed to be 'definitive' while actually being undiscriminating, we will see a series of pared-down, sharpened up 'studies'. Instead of speaking in a booming, pedagogic voice, the new biography will ask the reader to decide. Consuming this new biography may not be such a cosy experience, but it will bring us closer than ever to the real feeling of being alive.

34 What is the 'cultural transition' referred to in line 3?

    A   the scholarship exemplified in the best biographies
    B   the change in taste among ordinary readers
    C   the rising importance of sales figures in publishing
    D   the range of books available for purchase

35 In the second paragraph, what explanation is given for the current interest in biography?

    A   the range of subject matter in novels
    B   the failure of fiction to appeal to the average reader
    C   the choice of unsuitable main characters in novels
    D   the lack of skill of certain novelists

36 What contrast does the writer draw between literary novels and biography?

    A   Biography has dealt with more straightforward issues.
    B   Literary novels have presented a different type of truth.
    C   Biography has described a longer period in a person's life.
    D   Literary novels have been written in a more universal style.

37 In describing the work of Dyer, the writer

    A   underestimates his difficulties.
    B   makes fun of his efforts.
    C   acknowledges his expertise.
    D   is inspired by his achievements.

38 What is the writer's opinion of 'partial biography' (line 55)?

    A   It can provide new insights.
    B   It tends to remain inconclusive.
    C   It works when the subject is sufficiently interesting.
    D   It can detract from fuller studies.

39 What trend is exemplified by *Longitude* and *The Perfect Storm*?

    A   the fact that readers like complex puzzles
    B   the lack of interest generated by single lives
    C   the continuing sympathy towards human struggle
    D   the need to take account of the wider environment

40 Considering the future of biography, the writer anticipates

    A   a decline in the standard of biographical investigation.
    B   a greater challenge to the reading public.
    C   an improvement in the tone adopted by biographers.
    D   the growth of a new readership for biography.

PAPER 2 WRITING (2 hours)

Part 1

You **must** answer this question. Write your answer in **300–350** words in an appropriate style.

1 You have read the following extract from a letter to your local newspaper. You decide to write a letter to the newspaper, responding to the points raised and expressing your own views.

> I think that overall things are pretty easy for most young people these days. Our homes are full of labour-saving devices, so cooking and cleaning no longer take up a lot of time. And there are far more opportunities for study, travel and leisure than when we were young. Mind you, I'm not sure whether young people are any happier than we were, even though they have got so much ...

Write your **letter**. Do not write any addresses.

Part 2

Write an answer to **one** of the questions **2–5** in this part. Write your answer in **300–350** words in an appropriate style.

---

2   An international sports magazine has invited readers to submit articles to a special edition. Write an article describing the physical qualities you think are necessary to succeed in sports, and commenting on the extent to which participating in sports can develop certain mental qualities.

   Write your **article**.

3   Your local radio station wants to put on a two-hour programme for young people on weekday evenings, and has invited listeners to send in their proposals on what they think would be the most successful type of programme. You decide to submit a proposal giving your ideas on possible content, programme structure and style of presentation.

   Write your **proposal**.

4   A film festival is taking place in your town. The theme is:

   ### Comedy in the cinema – the films that make us laugh

   The organisers have asked filmgoers to write in with suggestions of films for the festival. Write a letter recommending a film that has made you laugh and saying why it should be shown at the festival.

   Write your **letter**. Do not write any addresses.

5   Based on your reading of **one** of these books, write on **one** of the following:

   (a)   Chinua Achebe: *Things Fall Apart*
   'We have brought a peaceful administration to you and your people, so that you may be happy.' Write an essay for your tutor describing the impact of the missionaries and the new administration on Okonkwo's life and assessing their role in his death.

   Write your **essay**.

   (b)   Ann Patchett: *Bel Canto*
   An arts magazine is planning a series of articles by readers entitled 'Falling in Love in Dangerous Circumstances'. You decide to submit an article on how the dangers surrounding Gen and Carmen in *Bel Canto* influence the development of their relationship.

   Write your **article**.

   (c)   J.B. Priestley: *An Inspector Calls*
   Your college magazine is running a series on crime stories with a difference, and has asked readers to send in letters on this theme. You decide to write a letter about *An Inspector Calls* stating how the play is different from other crime stories, given that the case the Inspector is investigating deals with moral crime rather than any other kind of crime.

   Write your **letter**. Do not write any addresses.

PAPER 3   USE OF ENGLISH (1 hour 30 minutes)

Part 1

For questions **1–15**, read the text below and think of the word which best fits each space. Use only **one** word in each space. There is an example at the beginning **(0)**.

Write your answers in CAPITAL LETTERS **on the separate answer sheet**.

Example: **0** M U C H

Urban Sparrows

During the last 25 years, Britain's urban sparrow population has declined by as **(0)**..MUCH.. as two-thirds, and the bird has almost disappeared from many of **(1)**............ former haunts. The decline has been blamed on **(2)**............ from cats to garden pesticides. Moreover, modern buildings have far **(3)**............ few nooks and crannies **(4)**............ the birds can nest. Factors **(5)**............ these may well be involved, but alone they **(6)**............ to explain the severity of the decline, or the fact that other urban birds have been less affected.

Denis Summers-Smith is the world's leading expert on sparrows, so when he **(7)**............ up with a theory to explain their decline, it has to be **(8)**............ listening to. He suggests that the culprit is a chemical added to unleaded petrol. It would be deeply ironic if a policy that was intended to improve the nation's health **(9)**............ to prove responsible for the decline of **(10)**............ of its favourite species.

(11)............ to Summers-Smith, social species such as the sparrow require a minimum population in a specific area to breed successfully. If, **(12)**............ whatever reason, numbers drop **(13)**............ this threshold, the stimulus to breed disappears. The most dramatic example is the passenger pigeon, **(14)**............ in the late nineteenth century went from **(15)**............ the world's most common bird to total extinction within 50 years.

Part 2

For questions **16–25**, read the text below. Use the word given in capitals at the end of some of the lines to form a word that fits in the space in the same line. There is an example at the beginning **(0)**.

Write your answers in CAPITAL LETTERS **on the separate answer sheet**.

Example: | 0 | T | W | E | N | T | I | E | T | H | | | | | | |

The Meaning of Dreams

Until the early **(0)**....TWENTIETH.... century, most scientists argued that dreams   **TWENTY**

were nothing but a random jumble of completely **(16)**............ images   **COMPREHEND**

remaining from the sensory accumulation of our daily lives. Since the idea that

dreams have meaning in their own way became popular, **(17)**............ have   **PSYCHOLOGY**

proposed **(18)**............ theories to explain the logic of dreams.   **COUNT**

The bewildering nature of this logic reflects the primary source of the dreams

outside the tidy confines of the conscious mind. A dream can be a response to

events in the outside world, or it can **(19)**............ within, expressing aspects of   **ORIGIN**

the dreamer's deep-seated feelings; it can fulfil desires or highlight unresolved

emotions in the dreamer's life. Not **(20)**............ , the contradictions implicit   **EXPECT**

in these complex processes are reflected in the syntax of dreams. Often

(21)............ , halting and fragmentary, the language of dreams can warp time,   **ENIGMA**

bringing together historical and contemporary figures. It can mix the familiar

with the **(22)**............ , and work fantastic transformations by its own brand of   **KNOW**

magic. Scenes in dreams merge **(23)**............ into one another, as in certain   **MYSTERY**

movies. People or animals may fly or inanimate things may move

(24)............ and talk. It is out of such complex and contrary   **DEPEND**

(25)............ that the meanings of dreams have to be teased.   **HAPPEN**

Part 3

For questions **26–31**, think of **one** word only which can be used appropriately in all three sentences. Here is an example **(0)**.

Example:

0 Some of the tourists are hoping to get compensation for the poor state of the hotel, and I think they have a very .... case.

There's no point in trying to wade across the river, the current is far too ....

If you're asking me which of the candidates should get the job, I'm afraid I don't have any .... views either way.

0	S	T	R	O	N	G														

Write **only** the missing word in CAPITAL LETTERS **on the separate answer sheet**.

---

26 Katerina must have reached New York by now, but there's been no .... from her yet.

Give me your .... that you won't forget to look me up when you next visit London.

When you see the boss, put in a good .... for me as I'm hoping for a pay rise.

27 We left early and so .... the rush hour traffic.

When he was at school, Simon never .... an opportunity to boast about his achievements.

Petra completely .... the point of what the lecturer had said and so asked an entirely inappropriate question.

28 The house was furnished with great ....

Having acquired a .... for the good life, Maria found it hard to settle at home again.

I strongly felt that the remarks Michael made at the party lacked ....

29   After taking the medicine, it's recommended that you wait a .... hour before eating.

It was gratifying that a .... number of people turned up for the director's farewell party.

.... intentions are all very well, but it's action that's required.

30   Apples are in .... supply this winter because of the summer drought.

In the .... term, our company prospects look very promising.

Henry would have finished his explanation but Sarah cut him ....

31   Pressure of work .... Kostas from taking more than a week's holiday last year.

The secretary .... a record of everything that was said during the discussion.

Mr Wilson .... a dog for company as he really enjoyed going for long country walks.

Part 4

For questions **32–39**, complete the second sentence so that it has a similar meaning to the first sentence, using the word given. **Do not change the word given.** You must use between **three** and **eight** words, including the word given.

Here is an example **(0)**.

Example:

0 Do you mind if I watch you while you paint?

objection

Do you ……………………………………………………… you while you paint?

0	*have any objection to my watching*

Write **only** the missing words **on the separate answer sheet**.

---

32 Marta is of the opinion that her boss has accepted a job abroad.

rumoured

Acccording to Marta, her boss ……………………………………………………… a job abroad.

33 James never really expected the plan to be a success.

of

James had little ……………………………………………………… a success.

34 Louise is an expert in all aspects of the business except marketing.

exception

With ……………………………………………………… , Louise is an expert in all aspects of the business.

35   Niko really enjoys going for a swim every morning.

on

What Niko .... going for a swim every morning.

36   This new radio is not at all similar to the previous model.

bears

This new radio .... the previous model.

37   Lydia went to London so that she could brush up her English.

reason

Lydia's .... that she wanted to brush up her English.

38   Managers intend to consult their staff about job descriptions.

are

Staff .... job descriptions by their managers.

39   It is quite obvious that we shall have to work faster in order to finish the project on time.

escaping

There is .... we shall have to work faster in order to finish the project on time.

Part 5

For questions **40–44**, read the following texts on cars. For questions **40–43**, answer with a word or short phrase. You do not need to write complete sentences. For question **44**, write a summary according to the instructions given.

Write your answers to questions **40–44 on the separate answer sheet**.

Many people in the western world consume half their lives, three-quarters of their energy and 99% of their emotions in travelling, without once using their legs and, arguably, without ever really getting anywhere; and no one seems to stop for long enough to ask why. 'The pedestrian remains the largest single obstacle to free traffic movement,' a Los Angeles planning officer reportedly once said. It's an attitude which typifies 20th-century urban planning in the western world and goes a long way towards explaining why so many cities are dominated by cars.

line 4

line 5

The inevitable result is a world where the motor car rules supreme; one with cities hemmed in by ring roads and flyovers, with sprawling suburbs where nobody walks and residents must drive endless kilometres for work or nourishment. In such an environment, children no longer play outside their houses or walk to school; people no longer stroll along the street or stand outside talking to the neighbours. Pedestrians have all but disappeared from the streets – and walking from the culture.

Moreover, people seem to live in complete awe of the device to which they have surrendered their lives, despite knowing that it denies them the clean air, peace and quiet and a pleasant living environment they claim to value so highly. It must have something to do with the fact that, once inside, they enjoy the unreal sense of power that comes from a complete surrender to mechanism. For although I'm not alone in regarding the car as a fearsome engine of destruction, nobody seems prepared to give it up.

40 In your own words, explain what the Los Angeles planning officer meant in the statement quoted in lines 4–5.

....

41 Which noun, used in the third paragraph, is intended as an indirect reference to the motor car?

....

Traffic congestion in Britain could be eased if it weren't for the nation's addiction to the absurd cult of the lone driver. But let's face it, sharing cars is something the British just don't do. Next Monday morning the streets will be overflowing with cars once again, most with spare seats front and back, and there will be few lifts on offer for those friends or colleagues who have no choice but to trudge through fumes or jostle in bus queues.

Many drivers, it seems, echo the view of one former transport minister who observed, albeit light-heartedly, that with cars 'you have your own company, your own temperature control and your own choice of music – and you don't have to put up with dreadful human beings sitting alongside you.' Many a true word, it seems, is said in jest. Indeed, sharing would threaten the very independence that makes the car such an attractive option in the first place. Offer a colleague a regular lift and you're locked into a routine as oppressive as any other, with all individual flexibility lost. So, what's in it for the driver?

But even in a motor-obsessed city such as Los Angeles, drivers have been won over by the idea of car-sharing. It is attractive because cars with more than one occupant are allowed access to fast-moving priority lanes. So desirable are these amid the six lanes of jam-packed traffic that, in the early days, Californian students charged motorists several dollars a time to pick them up.

42   Which word from the text best reveals the writer's personal view of British attitudes to the motor car?

....

43   In your own words, explain what is illustrated by the example of Los Angeles in the third paragraph of this text.

....

44   In a paragraph of **50–70** words, summarise **in your own words as far as possible** the reasons given in **both** texts to explain the continuing popularity of the motor car as a form of transport. Write your summary **on the separate answer sheet**.

PAPER 4 LISTENING (40 minutes approximately)

Part 1

You will hear four different extracts. For questions **1–8**, choose the answer (**A**, **B** or **C**) which fits best according to what you hear. There are two questions for each extract.

Extract One

You hear a man talking about his hobby, studying waterfalls.

1 In describing waterfalls, the speaker stresses that they

    A tend to behave unpredictably.
    B fit into one of a number of categories.
    C are more interesting to watch than listen to.

                                            1

2 What does he study in order to locate seasonal waterfalls?

    A rainfall patterns
    B features of the landscape
    C photographic evidence

                                            2

Extract Two

You hear a professor of Art History being interviewed about the restoration of old paintings.

3 In the professor's view, what can restorers achieve with an old painting?

    A They can return it to what it looked like originally.
    B They can only arrest the process of deterioration.
    C They can uncover some of its original vitality.

                                            3

4 According to the professor, some people want to leave old paintings as they are, due to

    A the risks involved in intervention.
    B contemporary thinking about art.
    C the limitations of scientific know-how.

                                            4

Extract Three

You hear part of a business programme about John Dixon, who invented a new type of vacuum cleaner.

5 According to the speaker, John's success is the result of his

   A   marketing strategy.
   B   design of the product.
   C   faith in the product.

6 The view of most business people is that manufacturing

   A   is out of date.
   B   is in decline.
   C   is wasteful of resources.

Extract Four

You hear part of a radio programme in which the subject of dust is being discussed.

7 What aspect of dust does the speaker begin by stressing?

   A   its insignificance
   B   its elusiveness
   C   its pervasiveness

8 What type of work is being reviewed?

   A   a popular science book
   B   a documentary film
   C   a photographic exhibition

Part 2

You will hear part of a lecture on the subject of jellyfish. For questions **9–17**, complete the sentences with a word or short phrase.

In appearance, the jellyfish is described as resembling two

	9

Because of their composition, jellyfish are largely without

	10

Very few adult jellyfish are alive in

	11

as they rarely survive for more than one year.

Tidal movements and the effects of

	12

determine where jellyfish can go in the sea.

Both jellyfish and people tend to end up in the sheltered bays where

	13

are formed.

The body of a box jellyfish can be as large as a

	14

Box jellyfish are not easy to see in water which is both

	15

and sunlit.

After being stung by a jellyfish, victims should avoid doing anything which makes their

	16

increase.

In the dark, the

	17

of the blue-coloured moon jellyfish appear to be glowing.

Part 3

You will hear part of an interview with Hal Jordan, who has recently written a book on the history of music. For questions **18–22**, choose the answer (**A**, **B**, **C** or **D**) which fits best according to what you hear.

18   According to Hal Jordan, what is the disadvantage of using computer programmes when writing music?

    A   Composers may be tempted to experiment too much.
    B   Composers have become too self-critical.
    C   Composers have become too reliant on machines.
    D   Composers may be dissatisfied with the results.

    18

19   Hal Jordan thinks that getting a computer to select the notes in a composition is

    A   a labour-saving device.
    B   a way to increase the sensitivity of the human ear.
    C   an idea that leads nowhere.
    D   an undemanding form of entertainment.

    19

20   One result of the invention of sound recording, according to Hal Jordan, was that

    A   people began to reassess familiar pieces of music.
    B   concert audiences slowly began to decline.
    C   the number of different music styles decreased.
    D   people disliked the unusual music they heard.

    20

21   According to Hal Jordan, how did the development of notation change Western music?

    A   It helped performers to develop their individual styles.
    B   It allowed for greater complexity of musical form.
    C   It encouraged composers to work more closely with musicians.
    D   It gave rise to the need for skilled music instructors.

    21

22   According to Hal Jordan, jazz is an example of

    A   pure spontaneity in modern music.
    B   a mixture of different approaches to music-making.
    C   music which is even less structured than it seems.
    D   the confusion which arises from improvisation.

    22

Part 4

You will hear two colleagues, Tina and Harry, talking about the problems of traffic congestion in their city. For questions **23–28**, decide whether the opinions are expressed by only one of the speakers, or whether the speakers agree.

Write: **T** for Tina,
         H for Harry,
or   **B** for Both, where they agree.

---

23 Personal experience suggests that the new bus-lane system has been ineffective in reducing traffic congestion.

       23

24 The bus-lane system may eventually encourage increased use of the buses.

       24

25 People resent the idea of losing the freedom that the motor car represents.

       25

26 Problems of traffic congestion actually restrict certain types of personal freedom.

       26

27 Some people have more reason to depend on their cars than others.

       27

28 By organising our everyday lives better, we would all cut down on car journeys.

       28

PAPER 5   SPEAKING (19 minutes)

There are two examiners. One (the interlocutor) conducts the test, providing you with the necessary materials and explaining what you have to do. The other examiner (the assessor) will be introduced to you, but then takes no further part in the interaction.

Part 1 (3 minutes)

The interlocutor first asks you and your partner a few questions which focus on information about yourselves and personal opinions.

Part 2 (4 minutes)

In this part of the test you and your partner are asked to talk together. The interlocutor places a set of pictures on the table in front of you. There may be only one picture in the set or as many as seven pictures. This stimulus provides the basis for a discussion. The interlocutor first asks an introductory question which focuses on two of the pictures (or in the case of a single picture, on aspects of the picture). After about a minute, the interlocutor gives you both a decision-making task based on the same set of pictures.

The pictures for Part 2 are on pages C8–C9 of the colour section.

Part 3 (12 minutes)

You are each given the opportunity to talk for two minutes, to comment after your partner has spoken and to take part in a more general discussion.

The interlocutor gives you a card with a question written on it and asks you to talk about it for two minutes. After you have spoken, your partner is first asked to comment and then the interlocutor asks you both another question related to the topic on the card. This procedure is repeated, so that your partner receives a card and speaks for two minutes, you are given an opportunity to comment and a follow-up question is asked.

Finally, the interlocutor asks some further questions, which leads to a discussion on a general theme related to the subjects already covered in Part 3.

The cards for Part 3 are on pages C5 and C10 of the colour section.

Paper 5 frames

Test 1

Note: In the examination, there will be both an assessor and an interlocutor in the room.

The visual material for Part 2 is on pages C2 and C3 in the colour section of the Student's Book. The prompt cards for Part 3 are on pages C5 and C10 in the colour section of the Student's Book.

Part 1   (3 minutes)

Interlocutor: Good morning/afternoon/evening. My name is .... and this is my colleague .... And your names are .... ?

Candidates: ....

Interlocutor: Thank you. Could I have your mark sheets, please?

First of all, we'd like to know something about you.

Where are you from, (*Candidate A*)? And you, (*Candidate B*)?

Select a further question for each candidate:

- Why did you choose to study English?
- You said that you're from (*candidate's town*). What is the best thing about living there?
- Do many visitors come to (*candidate's town*)?
- What kind of work can people do in (*candidate's town*)?
- What part of your town is best for shopping?

Candidates
A & B: ....

Interlocutor: *Select a further question for each candidate:*

- We'd like to know something about the sports facilities where you live.
- Where do you enjoy spending your holidays? What do you do there?
- Could you tell us something about a typical festival in your country?
- What's the most interesting aspect of what you do at the moment?
- What kind of work would you like to do in the future?
- Which do you prefer, going to the theatre or to the cinema? ... (Why?)

Candidates
A & B: ....

Interlocutor:	Thank you. Now, we'd like to ask you what you think about one or two things.

*Select **one** or more questions for each candidate, as appropriate:*

- How ambitious are you?
- Do you think it's a good idea for young people to travel to other countries? … (Why?/Why not?)
- How important do you think it is to learn about other cultures and lifestyles? Why?
- Communications are so good now that we can get news from all over the world very quickly. Do you think this is always a good thing?
- Do you think that people will still buy or read newspapers in ten years' time?
- What do you think of mobile phones? … Do you think people use them too much?

Candidates A & B:	………………………………………………………………………
Interlocutor:	Thank you.

Part 2   (4 minutes)   *Photographic exhibition – Originality*

Interlocutor:	Now, in this part of the test you're going to do something together. Here are some pictures that show different aspects of originality.

Place picture sheet for Test 1 in front of the candidates.
*Select **two** of the pictures for the candidates to look at*.*

First, I'd like you to look at the pictures * and * and talk together about what mood the photographer wanted to capture.

You have about a minute for this, so don't worry if I interrupt you.

Candidates A & B:	[*One minute.*]
Interlocutor:	Thank you. Now look at all the pictures.

I'd like you to imagine that there is going to be a photographic exhibition on the theme of 'Originality'. All these pictures will be included in the exhibition.

Talk together about the different aspects of originality, or lack of originality, that are suggested by these pictures. Then decide which one image should be used to advertise the exhibition.

You have about three minutes to talk about this.

Candidates A & B:	[*Three minutes.*]
Interlocutor:	Thank you. *Retrieve picture sheet.*

Part 3   (12 minutes)   *Education*

Interlocutor:	Now, in this part of the test you're each going to talk on your own for about two minutes. You need to listen while your partner is speaking because you'll be asked to comment afterwards.
	So, (*Candidate A*), I'm going to give you a card with a question written on it and I'd like you to tell us what you think. There are also some ideas on the card for you to use if you like.
	All right? Here is your card, and a copy for you, (*Candidate B*).
	Hand over a copy of prompt card 1a to each candidate.
	Remember, (*Candidate A*), you have about two minutes to talk before we join in.
	[*Allow up to 10 seconds before saying, if necessary:* Would you like to begin now?]
Candidate A:	[*Two minutes.*]
Interlocutor:	Thank you.
	*Select **one** appropriate response question for Candidate B:*
	• What do you think? • Is there anything you would like to add? • Is there anything you don't agree with? • How does this differ from your experience?
Candidate B:	[*One minute.*]
Interlocutor:	*Address **one** of the following follow-up questions to both candidates:*
	• Are teachers in your country respected? • Is there too much pressure on school children to succeed? • How can computers help with learning?
Candidates A & B:	[*One minute.*]
Interlocutor:	Thank you. *Retrieve cards.*
	Now, (*Candidate B*), it's your turn to be given a question.
	Hand over a copy of prompt card 1b to both candidates.
	Here is your card, and a copy for you, (*Candidate A*). Remember, (*Candidate B*), you have about two minutes to tell us what you think, and there are some ideas on the card for you to use if you like. All right?
	[*Allow up to 10 seconds before saying, if necessary:* Would you like to begin now?]
Candidate B:	[*Two minutes.*]
Interlocutor:	Thank you.

*Select **one** appropriate follow-up question for Candidate A:*

- What do you think?
- Is there anything you would like to add?
- Is there anything you don't agree with?
- How does this differ from your experience?

Candidate A: [*One minute.*]

Interlocutor: *Address **one** of the following follow-up questions to both candidates:*

- Is it possible to learn from other people's mistakes?
- What is the attraction of non-fiction books?
- Which book have you learnt most from?

Candidates
A & B: [*One minute.*]

Interlocutor: Thank you. *Retrieve cards.*

Interlocutor: Now, to finish the test, we're going to talk about 'education' in general.

Address a selection of the following questions to both candidates:

- What stops people from learning successfully?
- What about parents? What role should they play in a child's education?
- What can parents learn from their children?
- Is it possible to learn a foreign language successfully without learning about the culture?
- Some people say we never stop learning. To what extent do you agree?
- If you could travel back in time, which period would interest you? … Why?

Candidates
A & B: [*Up to four minutes.*]

Interlocutor: Thank you. That is the end of the test.

Test 2

Note: In the examination, there will be both an assessor and an interlocutor in the room.

The visual material for Part 2 is on page C4 in the colour section of the Student's Book. The prompt cards for Part 3 are on pages C5 and C10 in the colour section of the Student's Book.

Part 1   (3 minutes)

Interlocutor: Good morning/afternoon/evening. My name is ……… and this is my colleague ……… . And your names are ……… ?

Candidates: …………………………………   …………………………………

Interlocutor:	Thank you. Could I have your mark sheets, please?
	First of all, we'd like to know something about you.
	Where are you from, (*Candidate A*)? And you, (*Candidate B*)?
	Select a further question for each candidate:

- Are you in full-time study at the moment?
- Which aspect of your studies interests you most?
- Do you have any special interests outside your studies?
- Do you have any definite plans for the future?
- What do you like most about where you're living at present?

Candidates A & B:	....
Interlocutor:	*Select a further question for each candidate:*

- Could you tell us something about the kind of entertainment you enjoy?
- What opportunities are there for listening to live music where you live?
- What is the most memorable place you've ever visited?
- What do you find is the best way to keep fit?
- Do you see yourself as an independent person?
- If you could possess a very special talent, what would it be?

Candidates A & B:	....
Interlocutor:	Thank you. Now, we'd like to ask you what you think about one or two things.
	*Select **one** or more questions for each candidate, as appropriate:*

- What do you think is the best way to learn a new language?
- When it comes to protecting the environment, what can individuals do to help?
- Do you find that travelling is an enjoyable experience?
- Do you think that young people today share a similar outlook on life?
- Do you think that we are becoming too dependent on technology?
- Do you prefer saving or spending money?

Candidates A & B:	....
Interlocutor:	Thank you.

Part 2   (4 minutes)   *Computer magazine article – Play it Safe!*

Interlocutor:	Now, in this part of the test you're going to do something together. Here is a picture of a laptop computer.
	Place picture sheet for Test 2 in front of the candidates.
	First, I'd like you to look at the picture and talk together about your reactions to the chains on the computer.
	You have about a minute for this, so don't worry if I interrupt you.
Candidates A & B:	[*One minute.*]
Interlocutor:	Thank you. Now look at the picture again.
	I'd like you to imagine that a computer magazine has chosen this picture to illustrate an article entitled 'Play it Safe!'.
	Talk together about the possible dangers for computer users which should be highlighted in the article. Then suggest one further picture to illustrate the danger that you consider to be the most serious.
	You have about three minutes to talk about this.
Candidates A & B:	[*Three minutes.*]
Interlocutor:	Thank you. *Retrieve picture sheet.*

Part 3   (12 minutes)   *Living together*

Interlocutor:	Now, in this part of the test you're each going to talk on your own for about two minutes. You need to listen while your partner is speaking because you'll be asked to comment afterwards.
	So, (*Candidate A*), I'm going to give you a card with a question written on it and I'd like you to tell us what you think. There are also some ideas on the card for you to use if you like.
	All right? Here is your card, and a copy for you, (*Candidate B*).
	Hand over a copy of prompt card 2a to each candidate.
	Remember, (*Candidate A*), you have about two minutes to talk before we join in.
	[*Allow up to 10 seconds before saying, if necessary:* Would you like to begin now?]
Candidate A:	[*Two minutes.*]
Interlocutor:	Thank you.

*Select **one** appropriate response question for Candidate B:*

- What do you think?
- Is there anything you would like to add?
- Is there anything you don't agree with?
- How does this differ from your experience?

Candidate B: [*One minute.*]

Interlocutor: *Address **one** of the following follow-up questions to both candidates:*

- Do you think people were more socially responsible in the past?
- Should we as individuals be expected to take care of the neighbourhood we live in?
- Do you consider yourself to be a responsible person?

Candidates
A & B: [*One minute.*]

Interlocutor: Thank you. *Retrieve cards.*

Now, (*Candidate B*), it's your turn to be given a question.

Hand over a copy of prompt card 2b to both candidates.

Here is your card, and a copy for you, (*Candidate A*). Remember, (*Candidate B*), you have about two minutes to tell us what you think, and there are some ideas on the card for you to use if you like. All right?

[*Allow up to 10 seconds before saying, if necessary:* Would you like to begin now?]

Candidate B: [*Two minutes.*]

Interlocutor: Thank you.

*Select **one** appropriate response question for Candidate A:*

- What do you think?
- Is there anything you would like to add?
- Is there anything you don't agree with?
- How does this differ from your experience?

Candidate A: [*One minute.*]

Interlocutor: *Address **one** of the following follow-up questions to both candidates:*

- When is it more efficient to work alone?
- How important is it to work with people of different ages?
- Do you value colleagues at work as much as friends?

Candidates
A & B: [*One minute.*]

Interlocutor: Thank you. *Retrieve cards.*

Interlocutor:	Now, to finish the test, we're going to talk about 'living together' in general.

Address a selection of the following questions to both candidates:

- What are the advantages of living closely with others?
- Why do some people reject the society they were brought up in?
- What kind of events bring a community together? ... Does this coming together last?
- Thinking of the world as a whole, what do you think could be done to improve international understanding?
- What would be your ideal society?
- Do you expect the structure of family life to change? ... (How?)

Candidates A & B:	[*Up to four minutes.*]
Interlocutor:	Thank you. That is the end of the test.

Test 3

Note: In the examination, there will be both an assessor and an interlocutor in the room.

The visual material for Part 2 is on pages C6 and C7 in the colour section of the Student's Book. The prompt cards for Part 3 are on pages C5 and C10 in the colour section of the Student's Book.

Part 1 (3 minutes)

Interlocutor:	Good morning/afternoon/evening. My name is .... and this is my colleague .... And your names are .... ?
Candidates:	....
Interlocutor:	Thank you. Could I have your mark sheets, please?

First of all, we'd like to know something about you.

Where are you from, (*Candidate A*)? And you, (*Candidate B*)?

Select a further question for each candidate:

- What are you doing at present?
- Are you living at home or away from home?
- And do you live in a friendly neighbourhood?
- How important is English to you?
- Have you enjoyed any special event this year?

Candidates A & B:	....
Interlocutor:	*Select a further question for each candidate:*

- Is sport important in your life?
- Do you find that the internet is useful to you in your studies?

- Do you have a favourite celebrity?
- What is the most enjoyable thing about being a student?
- In your opinion, is it worthwhile reading newspapers and magazines?
- Can you tell us something about the schools you have attended?

Candidates
A & B: ....

Interlocutor: Thank you. Now, we'd like to ask you what you think about one or two things.

*Select **one** or more questions for each candidate, as appropriate:*

- Do you think it's a good idea for students to take a gap year?
- Most people live in cities nowadays. Is this a good thing in your opinion?
- If you had the chance to travel anywhere in the world, where would you go?
- Talking of television, are standards of programmes getting better or worse?
- In your opinion, do people spend too much time and money shopping?
- Do you think that people understand the importance of healthy food?

Candidates
A & B: ....

Interlocutor: Thank you.

Part 2 (4 minutes)   *Bank poster – Saving for old age*

Interlocutor: Now, in this part of the test you're going to do something together. Here are some pictures of elderly people.

Place picture sheet for Test 3 in front of the candidates.
*Select **two** of the pictures for the candidates to look at*.*

First, I'd like you to look at pictures * and * and talk together about how typical these activities are for elderly people.

You have about a minute for this, so don't worry if I interrupt you.

Candidates
A & B: [*One minute.*]

Interlocutor: Thank you. Now look at all the pictures.

I'd like you to imagine that a bank is producing a poster to encourage its customers to save for old age.

Talk together about the different aspects of old age that the pictures illustrate. Then decide which image would be most appropriate for the poster.

You have about three minutes to talk about this.

Candidates A & B:	[*Three minutes.*]
Interlocutor:	Thank you. *Retrieve picture sheet.*

Part 3 (12 minutes)   *Being at the centre*

Interlocutor: Now, in this part of the test you're going to talk on your own for about two minutes. You need to listen while your partner is speaking because you'll be asked to comment afterwards.

So, (*Candidate A*), I'm going to give you a card with a question written on it and I'd like you to tell us what you think. There are also some ideas on the card for you to use if you like.

All right? Here is your card, and a copy for you, (*Candidate B*).

Hand over a copy of prompt card 3a to each candidate.

Remember, (*Candidate A*), you have about two minutes to talk before we join in.

[*Allow up to 10 seconds before saying, if necessary:* Would you like to begin now?]

Candidate A: [*Two minutes.*]

Interlocutor: Thank you.

Select **one** *appropriate response question for Candidate B:*

- What do you think?
- Is there anything you would like to add?
- Is there anything you don't agree with?
- How does this differ from your experience?

Candidate B: [*One minute.*]

Interlocutor: *Address* **one** *of the following follow-up questions to both candidates:*

- What are the disadvantages of living in capital cities?
- Should salaries be higher in capital cities … (Why/Why not?)
- Do you think people living in capital cities are typical of their country?

Candidates A & B: [*One minute.*]

Interlocutor: Thank you. *Retrieve cards.*

Now, (*Candidate B*), it's your turn to be given a question.

Hand over a copy of prompt card 3b to both candidates.

Here is your card, and a copy for you, (*Candidate A*). Remember, (*Candidate B*), you have about two minutes to tell us what you think, and there are some ideas on the card for you to use if you like. All right?

121

[*Allow up to 10 seconds before saying, if necessary:* Would you like to begin now?]

Candidate B: [*Two minutes.*]

Interlocutor: Thank you.

*Select **one** appropriate response question for Candidate A:*

- What do you think?
- Is there anything you would like to add?
- Is there anything you don't agree with?
- How does this differ from your experience?

Candidate A: [*One minute.*]

Interlocutor: *Address **one** of the following follow-up questions to both candidates:*

- What are the advantages of not being the centre of attention?
- Is it easier for a group to get attention than an individual?
- Are there times when you enjoy being the centre of attention?

Candidates
A & B: [*One minute.*]

Interlocutor: Thank you. *Retrieve cards.*

Interlocutor: Now, to finish the test, we're going to talk about 'being at the centre' in general.

Address a selection of the following questions to both candidates:

- In your experience, who has the central role in the family? ... Has this changed?
- Being at the centre is usually associated with being in control. Do you agree?
- Some people say that we have to be self-centred to survive today. What do you think?
- To what extent do you think our lives are dominated by work?
- In your/this country is the trend towards centralisation or decentralisation?
- What common interests do people in your/this country have? ... Do you share these?

Candidates
A & B: [*Up to four minutes.*]

Interlocutor: Thank you. That is the end of the test.

Test 4

Note: In the examination, there will be both an assessor and an interlocutor in the room.

The visual material for Part 2 is on pages C8 and C9 in the colour section of the Student's Book. The prompt cards for Part 3 are on pages C5 and C10 in the colour section of the Student's Book.

Part 1 (3 minutes)

Interlocutor:	Good morning/afternoon/evening. My name is .... and this is my colleague .... And your names are .... ?
Candidates:	....
Interlocutor:	Thank you. Could I have your mark sheets, please?
	First of all, we'd like to know something about you.
	Where are you from, (*Candidate A*)? And you, (*Candidate B*)?

Select a further question for each candidate:

- What do you do?
- What is your favourite type of English lesson?
- Do you think that you will use English for your work in the future?
- You said that you're from ... . Were you born there?
- Is ... an interesting place to live?

Candidates A & B:	....
Interlocutor:	*Select a further question for each candidate:*

- What time of the year do you enjoy most? ... (Why?)
- Can you tell us something about how you enjoy spending your evenings in the summer?
- We'd like to know something about public transport in the place where you live.
- What do you hope to be doing this time next year?
- What kind of job do you think would suit you best?
- Could you tell us something about your favourite types of film?

Candidates A & B:	....
Interlocutor:	Thank you. Now, we'd like to ask you what you think about one or two things.

*Select **one** or more questions for each candidate, as appropriate:*

- Do you think it is easier to learn new things alone, or with a teacher?
- Do you think that traditional skills like cooking are being lost nowadays? ... (How do you feel about this?)

- What is the best way of finding out about a place before you visit it?
- What effect do you think the weather has on a nation's personality and culture?
- Do you think that we have lost the art of entertaining ourselves nowadays?
- Do you think that people read more or less now than they used to?

Candidates
A & B: ....

Interlocutor: Thank you.

Part 2   (4 minutes)   *Posters for training courses – Achieving success*

Interlocutor: Now, in this part of the test you're going to do something together. Here are some pictures showing different situations.

Place picture sheet for Test 4 in front of the candidates.
*Select **two** of the pictures for the candidates to look at*.*

First, I'd like you to look at pictures * and * and talk together about why you think the photographs were taken.

You have about a minute for this, so don't worry if I interrupt you.

Candidates
A & B: [*One minute.*]

Interlocutor: Thank you. Now look at all the pictures.

I'd like you to imagine that a training organisation is producing a set of three posters to advertise its courses on achieving success.

Talk together about the different aspects of success shown in the pictures. Then decide which three pictures would be most effective for the posters advertising the courses.

You have about three minutes to talk about this.

Candidates
A & B: [*Three minutes.*]

Interlocutor: Thank you. *Retrieve picture sheet.*

Part 3   (12 minutes)   *Taste*

Interlocutor: Now, in this part of the test you're each going to talk on your own for about two minutes. You need to listen while your partner is speaking because you'll be asked to comment afterwards.

So, (*Candidate A*), I'm going to give you a card with a question written on it and I'd like you to tell us what you think. There are also some ideas on the card for you to use if you like.

All right? Here is your card, and a copy for you, (*Candidate B*).

Hand over a copy of prompt card 4a to each candidate.

Remember, (*Candidate A*), you have about two minutes to talk before we join in.

[*Allow up to 10 seconds before saying, if necessary:* Would you like to begin now?]

Candidate A: [*Two minutes.*]

Interlocutor: Thank you.

*Select **one** appropriate response question for Candidate B:*

- What do you think?
- Is there anything you would like to add?
- Is there anything you don't agree with?
- How does this differ from your experience?

Candidate B: [*One minute.*]

Interlocutor: *Address **one** of the following follow-up questions to both candidates:*

- Who decides what is a work of art?
- How significant is art in people's everyday lives?
- Which of the arts do you find most appealing?

Candidates
A & B: [*One minute.*]

Interlocutor: Thank you. *Retrieve cards.*

Now, (*Candidate B*), it's your turn to be given a question.

Hand over a copy of prompt card 4b to both candidates.

Here is your card, and a copy for you, (*Candidate A*). Remember, (*Candidate B*), you have about two minutes to tell us what you think, and there are some ideas on the card for you to use if you like. All right?

[*Allow up to 10 seconds before saying, if necessary:* Would you like to begin now?]

Candidate B: [*Two minutes.*]

Interlocutor: Thank you.

*Select **one** appropriate response question for Candidate A:*

- What do you think?
- Is there anything you would like to add?
- Is there anything you don't agree with?
- How does this differ from your experience?

Candidate A: [*One minute.*]

Interlocutor:	*Address **one** of the following follow-up questions to both candidates:*

- What is the connection between fashion and money?
- What are the advantages of uniforms?
- How international is fashion?

Candidates A & B:	[*One minute.*]
Interlocutor:	Thank you. *Retrieve cards.*

Interlocutor:	Now, to finish the test, we're going to talk about 'taste' in general.

Address a selection of the following questions to both candidates:

- To what extent do we judge people by their appearance?
- What do we mean by good taste? ... (Can it be learnt?)
- How easy is it to get on with people who have very different tastes from yourself?
- What makes out tastes change? ... (Do our tastes automatically change as we get older?)
- Some people say that cars reflect our personality. What do you think?
- What can we tell about a country from its architecture?

Candidates A & B:	[*Up to four minutes.*]
Interlocutor:	Thank you. That is the end of the test.

Marks and results

Paper 1   Reading

One mark is given for each correct answer in Part 1; two marks are given for each correct answer in Parts 2–4. The total score is then weighted to 40 marks for the whole Reading paper.

Paper 2   Writing

An impression mark is awarded to each piece of writing using the general mark scheme. Examiners use band descriptors to assess language and task achievement. Each piece of writing is assigned to a band between 0 and 5 and can be awarded one of three performance levels within that band. For example, in Band 4, 4.1 represents weaker performance within Band 4; 4.2 represents typical performance within Band 4; 4.3 represents strong performance within Band 4. Acceptable performance at CPE level is represented by a Band 3. All tasks carry the same maximum mark.

The general impression mark scheme is used in conjunction with a task-specific mark scheme, which focuses on content, range of structures, vocabulary, organisation, register and format and the effect on the target reader of a specific task.

American spelling and usage is acceptable.

Band 5	Outstanding realisation of the task set: • sophisticated use of an extensive range of vocabulary, collocation and expression, entirely appropriate to the task set • effective use of stylistic devices; register and format wholly appropriate • impressive use of a wide range of structures • skilfully organised and coherent • excellent development of topic • minimal error Impresses the reader and has a very positive effect.
Band 4	Good realisation of the task set: • fluent and natural use of a wide range of vocabulary, collocation and expression, successfully meeting the requirements of the task set • good use of stylistic devices; register and format appropriate • competent use of a wide range of structures • well organised and coherent • good development of topic • minor and unobtrusive errors Has a positive effect on the reader.

	Satisfactory realisation of the task set:
Band 3	• reasonably fluent and natural use of a range of vocabulary and expression, adequate to the task set • evidence of stylistic devices; register and format generally appropriate • adequate range of structures • clearly organised and generally coherent • adequate coverage of topic • some non-impeding errors Achieves the desired effect on the reader.
Band 2	Inadequate attempt at the task set: • limited and/or inaccurate range of vocabulary and expression • little evidence of stylistic devices; some attempt at appropriate register and format • inadequate range of structures • some attempt at organisation, but lacks coherence • inadequate development of topic • a number of errors, which sometimes impede communication Has a negative effect on the reader.
Band 1	Poor attempt at the task set: • severely limited and inaccurate range of vocabulary and expression • no evidence of stylistic devices; little or no attempt at appropriate register and format • lack of structural range • poorly organised, leading to incoherence • little relevance to topic, and/or too short • numerous errors, which distract and often impede communication Has a very negative effect on the reader.
Band 0	Negligible or no attempt at the task set: • incomprehensible due to serious error • totally irrelevant • insufficient language to assess (fewer than 20% of the required number of words – 60) • totally illegible

Paper 2 sample answers and examiner's comments

The following pieces of writing have been selected from students' answers. The samples relate to tasks in Tests 1–4. Explanatory notes have been added to show how the bands have been arrived at. The comments should be read in conjunction with the task-specific mark schemes included in the Keys.

Sample A (Test 1, Question 3)

Dear Sir/Madam

I am writing in response for your article about the cultural significance of food, which appeared on the 2nd December 2004.

 I believe that my country, Poland, is a perfect example for a place where food is of incredible importance. Since we are little children, we begin to acknowledge how much a loaf of bread means to our parents – to some it may sound silly but for me the custom of kissing bread before you start cutting it is simply amazing. It's not so common nowadays to worship food this way, since you hardly ever bake your own bread, and the one from the supermarket doesn't have a 'soul'. Besides, everyone would call you crazy if you tried to kiss every bread roll before you ate them! But despite the fact, that we no longer make our food 'from scratch', some customs have been preserved – that's why I feel so incredibly guilty every time I have to throw any food away – even though I have moved out of my parents' house over eight years ago and nobody would tell me off for this anymore! For the same reason the Poles invented all these really simple dishes that you make from leftovers – delicious, by the way.

 A fairly high percentage of our nation is still working as farmers, eating what they grow and harvest and therefore appreciating everything more – it's widely known that you value more anything that needed your effort in the first place. In most Polish homes, especially the one of farmers, the whole family would try and have their meals together – extremely difficult in present times, but so rewarding! You can catch up with other members' troubles and successes, give your children some of your attention, generally – sit down for a moment instead of rushing through life aimlessly. Furthermore, your body, and digestive system in particular will be very grateful for this slower consumption!

 But food in Poland is not only to be eaten every day. Any special occasion, be it a wedding, Christmas, a birthday or even a funeral is celebrated with a lavish meal. Women in the house get together and cook, sometimes for a few days before, and the exceptionally good or unusual food will be remembered and commented on widely – no wonder little competitions between a mother and a daughter-in-law are so common!

 Our parents consider us ready for an adult life if they can see that we will not starve if left alone – and they would never count on ready-made supermarket meals or the chance that our partner will be a professional cook! 'Medieval customs', one might say, but I say – come to Poland and see it for yourselves!

 As you can see, you cannot overestimate the importance of food in Poland. What's more, virtually every Pole will be as enthusiastic about the topic as I am!

Yours faithfully

Comments

Content
Excellent development of topic.

Range
Impressive use of a wide range of structures.

Appropriacy of register and format
Consistent and wholly appropriate.

Organisation and cohesion
Skilfully organised and coherent.

Accuracy
Minimal error.

Target reader
Impresses and interests the target reader.

Band 5

Sample B (Test 1, Question 5b)

L.P. Hartley, on his novel The *Go-Between* introduces us to Leo. He is a young boy, just about to turn thirteen, who is invited to his schoolfriends house to spend part of the summer holiday. The author uses Leo's character to introduces us to a middle class family who are eager to marry their daugther with aristocratic Lord Trimingham.

From the moment of his arrival to Brandham Hall, Leo is chosen by Marian, daughter of his host to be her "postman". Leo, overwhelmed by her attention he soon agrees to carry out the duty of emisary. Through Marian, Leo is introduced to Lord Trimingham and Ted Burgess, the former being a farmer living in the county.

Although from very different backgrounds, both welcome Leo's character to court Marian. Lord Trimingham takes the opportunity to ask Leo to deliver messages to his love, whilst, Ted Burgess also requests him to deliver messages to his lover.

In this novel, Lord Trimingham comprises what the society at the time saw invaluable, such as position, land and wealth. On the other hand, Ted Burgess characters shows us emotions, such as passion and anger.

Throught the story Lord Trimingham addresses Leo with propriety. He is treated as a child who knows little about the facts of live. However when encountered by Ted's character, Leo experiences anger, when he first traspasses onto the grounds of the farm, as well as respect when he explains to Leo the meaning of "spooning".

Both characters, Trimingham and Burgess, welcome Leo; for Trimingham is a commodity, as he does not need to hide his feelings; but for Burgess is a necessity, as his status in society deprives him from ever being in a public relationship with Marian.

L.P Hartley, manages to give us all insight of middle class English society, where propriety is more important than emotions.

Comments

Content
Adequate coverage of the topic.

Range
Adequate range of structures.

Appropriacy of register and format
Generally appropriate.

Organisation and cohesion
Clearly organised and generally coherent.

Accuracy
Some non-impeding errors.

Target reader
Would learn something about the two characters and their attitudes towards Leo.

Band 3

Sample C (Test 2, Question 1)

It is an undisputable fact that computers have radically changed our lives since their first wide appearance some decades ago. In at least every aspect of our world, computers are present and their dominance cannot be denied by anyone. However, the intrusion of computers has raised many ethical questions, the most general and most important of which is whether computers are a blessing or a curse; whether they are our best friends or our worst enemies.

On the first hand, there are those who become fascinated about this exciting world. Technophiles you may call them, can easily be spotted by their most immediate reactions when confronted with a brand new piece of equipment or technological break-through. They tend to advocate that computers have substantially changed the way we live, think and act, even the ways we communicate, making it possible to contact anyone, no matter how far he may be, within fragments of a second. They believe that computers have opened a door to a range of endless possibilities.

On the other hand, there are technophobes; in other words, people who are afraid of technology and its consequences, recognised by the suspicion they radiate, when, for example, hear about a major scientific discovery on the news. Their opinion is that, having computers so much of the work that we used to do, will eventually render us unable to think and create, thus leading humanity to doom. They believe that computers will eventually aid to our destruction.

My own point is that both sides have an equal share of the truth. Computers are indeed one of the most important and innovative inventions ever devised, but wrong exploitation of their power could have dramatic effects. Many feats of mankind, such as landing on the moon, would not have been possible without extensive use of computers. However, over-relying on them to perform even the most basic of our activities, would result in the diminishing of our general abilities. We would fall asleep in some wonderful technological garden. It is laid on our species' wisdom to make the best use out of them.

Comments

Content
Good development of topic.

Range
Competent use of a wide range of structures and, particularly, of vocabulary, despite occasional lapses.

Appropriacy of register and format
Completely appropriate.

Organisation and cohesion
Well organised and coherent.

Accuracy
Generally accurate, but does have occasional minor errors.

Target reader
Positive effect.

Band 4

Sample D (Test 2, Question 1)

In nowadays computers have become the most usefull way at accessing to information. Many people believe that the frecuent use of computer may hide some serious dangers about our mind and our personality. Everyone from the youngest to the eldest have being sit in frond of a computer at least for one time.

There are of course many advantages by the use of a computer. First of all, we are able to have access to information on our incredible scale, at any time. The only thing that we have to do is to have access to the internet and just search for any kind of information we would like to know. Furthermore, we have the opportunity through computers, to contact people anywhere in the world. We can have chat, exchanging opinions and develop new friendships, learn about different cultures and civilisations. Also the opportunities that are to us by the use of computers are endless, we can get in an on-line shop and buy whatever we like and almost with the same cost as if we buy it from a store.

On the other hand there are serious consequences which might influence our personality. It is true that with computer we might make friends, but they are friends who probably we never see. e are able to do all out work fro our home and we don't have the chance to increase a more personal contact with others. This may result in a less social society. Also providing computers to us almost all the solutions to our problems we become slowly and surely, less hard-working, we just feel that we should not try for anything and this restrict our intelligence, producing lazy and careless personalities.

In conclusion it is obvious that the seriousness of the advantages and disadvantages of the computers must be considered. And the only thing that we have to do is just to not let ourselves being fully devoted to computers. And have in mind that it remains to be seen if computers are our best friend or worst enemy.

Comments

Content
Points covered.

Range
Attempts a range of structures.

Appropriacy of register and format
Satisfactory.

Organisation and cohesion
Some attempt at organisation, but lacks coherence at sentence level.

Accuracy
A number of errors which sometimes impede communication.

Target reader
Negative effect.

Band 2

Sample E (Test 3, Question 4)

I was greatly inspired by your very interesting and informative article about the wheel as our best invention. True, one does not realise how many things have stemmed from this single shapely object – we take them for granted. However, although the wheel may have been one of the first great inventions, but it was not the only one that has contributed to the development of our civilisation.

In my opinion the invention of paper has been equally significant. It does not matter that other great world civilisations, i.e. ancient China and Egypt were there first. It is the Western civilisation that has really used it fully and its current world position cannot be imagined without the invention of paper.

First of all, paper allowed people to record and preserve their thoughts. Human ideas were no longer elusive and temporary. They could be kept for others for a long time. This made it possible for science and culture to develop. Thanks to paper intra-cultural and international exchange of ideas could happen. Paper available to the highest strata of society stores the most important records: laws and orders, church liturgy, but also literature in many languages. People could develop a written form of the language they spoke. Every nation is proud of the earliest written records of their poets and writers' words. Paper made education possible to the scale earlier unimaginable.

Some may argue that print is an invention that added greatly to the invention of paper, but we should not forget which one was the first.

Thus, combined print and paper marked the beginning of civil society and democracy. Access to information – the Bible – and the fact that more and more people could learn to read and interpret a written word meant that everybody could judge for themselves and refused to obey orders of some higher authority that could simply be wrong. The development of printed documents is inextricably connected with modern capitalism and industrial society. Money first in the form of metal coins, soon took the shape of banknotes and other securities. We are not able to imagine the world without them now.

Paper is everywhere. It is something obvious and natural. It will not be replaced by any electronic devices. The vision of a workplace without paper, predicted some time ago, will never materialize. We may prefer to write an e-mail on our PC, but we will always enjoy a tactile pleasure of turning a page as we read.

Comments

Content
Outstanding realisation of the task set.

Range
Impressive use of a wide range.

Appropriacy of register and format
Wholly appropriate.

Organisation and cohesion
Skilfully organised and coherent.

Accuracy
Minimal error.

Target reader
Impresses the reader and has a very positive effect.

Band 5

Sample F (Test 4, Question 2)

The qualities of a successful athlete!

Do you believe that participating in sport helps people to develop mentally? Have you ever considered starting a professional career as an athlete? What qualifications and physical qualities would you need? Would it be too difficult to succeed in sports or would you face high competitiveness? I believe that those who become athletes are born athletes so I think that the qualities which are important are physical qualities and I am going to comment on them.

Firstly, I think that some physical qualities may be developed through continuing rigid, training and the main of these qualities are strength and stamina. On the other hand, many people are gifted with physical qualities from the time they are borne. Flair, physical features such as height and speed are innate skills and I believe that they can't be acquired and developed however hard one may try.

Considering the extent to which physical qualities are necessary in order to become a successful athlete, I tend to think that all of them are very important but modern sports set some basic requirements. For sports such as football, rugby and basketball, you need to be very talented and have a high level of physical skills, especially speed, strength and flexibility. However, for individual sports such as gymnastics and swimming, I believe that the qualities which are necessary are mainly mental, although you need to be very fit in order to be able to meet the demands of the hardest of contests.

In spite of the hard training which is needed, the athletes have the chance to develop their mental qualities by taking part in sports so I believe that being an athlete is worthy at all costs. I think that the majority of athletes boost their self-confidence when they finally see that their efforts have been appreciated and they are awarded a medal if they win in a significant competition. I also believe that determination, passion, concentration and anticipation are basic qualities of sportspeople and they develop them even more through participating in sports.

So, what do you finally consider that being an athlete means? I thinks that it means a lot and you can pride yourself on being an athlete because it is very difficult to reach a professional level in sports. It is undeniable that physical skills are the main qualities for sports and that you can have a go at a sport activity because even if you don't take it up professionally it is a really constructive activity. Are you still in doubt about taking sports seriously?

Comments

Content
Ambitious but not always successful realisation of the topic.

Range
Wide expression of range and vocabulary.

Appropriacy of register and format
Appropriate for a magazine article.

Organisation and cohesion
Well organised and coherent.

Accuracy
Minor and unobtrusive errors.

Target reader
Has a positive effect on the target reader.

Band 4

Paper 3   Use of English

One mark is given for each correct answer in Parts 1 and 2.
Two marks are given for each correct answer in Part 3.
Up to two marks may be awarded for each correct answer in Part 4.
Two marks are given for each correct answer in Part 5, questions 40–43.

Fourteen marks are available for Part 5, question 44. Up to four marks may be awarded for content (see test keys for content points) and ten for summary writing skills. The ten marks for summary writing skills are divided into five bands using the summary mark scheme below.

5.2 5.1	Outstanding realisation of the task set: • totally relevant • concise and totally coherent • skilfully organised, with effective use of linking devices • skilfully reworded, where appropriate • minimal non-impeding errors, probably due to ambition Clearly informs and requires no effort on the part of the reader.
4.2 4.1	Good realisation of the task set: • mostly relevant • concise and mostly coherent • well organised, with good use of linking devices • competently reworded, where appropriate • occasional non-impeding errors Informs and requires minimal or no effort on the part of the reader.
3.2 3.1	Satisfactory realisation of the task set: • generally relevant, with occasional digression • some attempt at concise writing and reasonably coherent • adequately organised, with some appropriate use of linking devices • adequately reworded, where appropriate • some errors, mostly non-impeding Adequately informs, though may require some effort on the part of the reader.
2.2 2.1	Inadequate attempt at the task set: • some irrelevance • little attempt at concise writing, so likely to be over-length and incoherent in places OR too short • some attempt at organisation, but only limited use of appropriate linking devices and may use inappropriate listing or note format • inadequately reworded and/or inappropriate lifting • a number of errors, which sometimes impede communication Partially informs, though requires considerable effort on the part of the reader.
1.2 1.1	Poor attempt at the task set: • considerable irrelevance • no attempt at concise writing, so likely to be seriously over-length and seriously incoherent OR far too short • poorly organised, with little or no use of appropriate linking devices and/or relies on listing or note format • poorly reworded and/or over-reliance on lifting • numerous errors, which distract and impede communication Fails to inform and requires excessive effort on the part of the reader.
0	Negligible or no attempt at the task set: • does not demonstrate summary skills • incomprehensible due to serious error • totally irrelevant • insufficient language to assess (fewer than 10 words) • totally illegible

Paper 3 summary answers and examiner's comments

The following pieces of writing have been selected from students' answers. The samples relate to question 44 in Tests 1–4. Explanatory notes have been added to show how the bands have been arrived at. The comments should be read in conjunction with the summary content points included in the Keys.

Sample A (Test 1)

> Firstly, contrary to what is believed, even if still-life paintings are representations of ordinary objects, they can have a huge impact on people.
>
> Moreover, they show the weight of time and space. Due to this fact, they are misterious and meaningful, and many people look for answers hidden beyond the strokes.
>
> Finally, still-life paintings are a means of showing the world from a unique and personal perspective, the artist's vision of the world.

Comments

Content points: (i), (ii)

This is a concise and satisfactory partial summary. The fact that it only covers two of the summary points limits the grade.

Content: 2 marks

Summary skills: Band 2

Sample B (Test 2)

> Climbing has even nowadays a great appeal to people due to the feeling of excitement it evokes and the adventure it offers. Ascending a mountain and exploring remote areas gives a feeling of achievement, selfawareness and the chance to enjoy the view. Reaching the summit gives the impression of reaching the sky, of conquering a place. At that moment the soul is full of enthusiasm and joy.

Comments

Content points: (i), (iii), (iv)

This summary is totally relevant, concise and skilfully organised. However, only three points are clearly made and the ideas are not very well linked.

Content: 3 marks

Summary skills: Band 4

Sample C (Test 3)

> Working out of home increase people dedication and concentration. It also enables to develop workers social life, making them to relax and forget about personal problems. Moreover, people perceive themselves as more valuable and independents. Finally, the division between work and home appears to be essential to keep our brains healthier and to earn estimation. The advantages are clear.

Comments

Content points: (i), (ii), (iii), (iv)

All four content points are covered but the fourth point is only just there. The summary adequately informs but includes numerous errors, some of which are impeding.

Content: 4 marks

Summary skills: Band 3

Sample D (Test 3)

> While going out to work provides the possibility to make a difference between home and work, which is vital for your psychological health, it also enables you to boost your self-confidence as it gives you a certain identity. Whereas for some people work is the key to community and interaction, other people, by contrast, regard it as an escape from difficult situations and social problems at home.

Comments

Content points: (i), (ii), (iii), (iv)

All four content points are covered. The summary is totally relevant, skilfully reworded and well organised. It informs clearly, and requires very little effort from the reader.

Content: 4 marks

Summary skills: Band 5

Sample E (Test 4)

> According to the first text, people spend a great part of their life driving a car. Most of the times they haven't got any reason for driving. It seems that they've put aside the idea of walking and pedestrians tend to disappear. Another reason is that they made car vital for their life. The second texts says that people prefer to drive alone and that leads to the fact that there is at least one car for every person.

Comments

Content points:

The summary does not identify any content points. It fails to inform and is mostly irrelevant.

Content: 0 marks

Summary skills: Band 1

Sample F (Test 4)

There are many reasons. First, the urban planning makes people to avoid going somewhere on foot. Second, motor car has become such a common device in people's lives that they can't stand living without it, even if they know that it deprives them of a pleasant living environment. Third, it makes people feel more independent apart from their habit to drive alone and not wanting to have someone sitting alongside. Moreover, people do not have to wait in queues or walk in fumes.

Comments

Content Points: (i), (iii), (iv)

The summary is well organised and reasonably coherent. However, there is some irrelevance and error, which limits the grade.

Content: 3 marks

Summary skills: Band 3

Paper 4   Listening

One mark is given for each correct answer. The total is weighted to give a mark out of 40 for the paper. In **Part 2** minor spelling errors are allowed, provided that the candidate's intention is clear.

For security reasons, several versions of the Listening paper are used at each administration of the examination. Before grading, the performance of the candidates in each of the versions is compared and marks adjusted to compensate for any imbalance in levels of difficulty.

Paper 5   Speaking

Assessment

Candidates are assessed on their own individual performance and not in relation to each other, according to the following five analytical criteria: grammatical resource, lexical resource, discourse management, pronunciation and interactive communication. These criteria are interpreted at CPE level. Assessment is based on performance in the whole test and is not related to particular parts of the test.

Both examiners assess the candidates. The assessor applies detailed, analytical scales, and the interlocutor applies the global achievement scale, which is based on the analytical scales.

Analytical scales

Grammatical resource

This refers to the accurate application of grammar rules and the effective arrangement of words in utterances. At CPE level a wide range of grammatical forms should be used appropriately and competently. Performance is viewed in terms of the overall effectiveness of the language used.

Lexical resource

This refers to the candidate's ability to use a wide and appropriate range of vocabulary to meet task requirements. At CPE level the tasks require candidates to express precise meanings, attitudes and opinions and to be able to convey abstract ideas. Performance is viewed in terms of the overall effectiveness of the language used.

Discourse management

This refers to the candidate's ability to link utterances together to form coherent monologue and contributions to dialogue. The utterances should be relevant to the tasks and to preceding utterances in the discourse. The discourse produced should be at a level of complexity appropriate to CPE level and the utterances should be arranged logically to develop the themes or arguments required by the tasks. The extent of contributions should be appropriate, i.e. long or short as required at a particular point in the dynamic development of the discourse in order to achieve the task.

Pronunciation

This refers to the candidate's ability to produce easily comprehensible utterances to fulfil the task requirements. At CPE level, acceptable pronunciation should be achieved by the appropriate use of strong and weak syllables, the smooth linking of words and the effective highlighting of information-bearing words. Intonation, which includes the use of a sufficiently wide pitch range, should be used effectively to convey meaning and articulation of individual sounds should be sufficiently clear for words to be understood. Examiners put themselves in the position of the non-EFL specialist and assess the overall impact of the communication and the degree of effort required to understand the candidate.

Interactive communication

This refers to the candidate's ability to take an active part in the development of the discourse, showing sensitivity to turn taking and without undue hesitation. It requires the ability to participate competently in the range of interactive situations in the test and to develop discussions on a range of topics by initiating and responding appropriately. It also refers to the deployment of strategies to maintain and repair interaction at an appropriate level throughout the test so that the tasks can be fulfilled.

Global achievement scale

This scale refers to the candidate's overall effectiveness in dealing with the tasks in the three parts of the CPE Speaking Test.

Marks

Marks for each scale are awarded out of five and are subsequently weighted to produce a final mark out of 40.

Test 1 Key

Paper 1   Reading (1 hour 30 minutes)

Part 1   (one mark for each correct answer)

1 D	2 A	3 A	4 B	5 D	6 C	7 D	8 A	9 C
10 B	11 C	12 B	13 D	14 D	15 B	16 B	17 A	
18 C								

Part 2   (two marks for each correct answer)

19 B	20 D	21 B	22 A	23 A	24 D	25 C	26 A

Part 3   (two marks for each correct answer)

27 G	28 H	29 F	30 C	31 D	32 A	33 E

Part 4   (two marks for each correct answer)

34 A	35 C	36 C	37 D	38 B	39 C	40 A

Paper 2   Writing (2 hours)

Task-specific mark schemes

Question 1: Studying History

Content
Article must discuss studying history with reference to
- the help it gives in understanding patterns in human behaviour and how and why things happen
- the idea that it is a waste of time
- the need to look to the future, not just the past

Range
Language for
- attacking/defending the arguments expressed
- expressing and supporting opinions

Appropriacy of register and format
Register consistently appropriate for an article in a magazine.

Organisation and cohesion
Clearly organised ideas.
Well-developed argument leading to a conclusion.

Target reader
Would understand
- the writer's response to the points raised
- the writer's own opinions about studying history

Question 2: Weekend Activities for Teenagers

Content
The proposal must explain and describe
- the reasons for setting up the group
- the aims of the group
- the proposed activities of the group

Range
Language for
- making proposals
- giving information
- justifying/persuading

Appropriacy of register and format
Register consistently appropriate for a proposal to a local council.
Proposal format, probably with headings.

Organisation and cohesion
Well-organised proposal.
An introduction – stating purpose of proposal.
A conclusion – which supports the reasons for the establishment of the group.

Target reader
Would
- understand what is proposed for the group
- consider supporting the scheme

Question 3: The Role of Food

Content
The letter must explain the role of food in the writer's region/country with reference to
- daily life
- customs and celebrations

Range
Language for
- giving information
- describing
- explaining
- analysing

Appropriacy of register and format
Register consistently appropriate for a letter to a magazine.

Organisation and cohesion
Clearly organised and paragraphed.
Introduction giving reason for writing, and appropriate conclusion.
Description leading to analysis and explanation.

Target reader
Would gain a good understanding of the role of food in daily life, customs and celebrations in the writer's region/country.

Question 4: Magazine Review

Content
The review must
- discuss the chosen magazine and
- evaluate some aspects, for example, use of colour and pictures, interesting articles, appeal to reader and value for money

Range
Language for
- describing
- evaluating

Appropriacy of register and format
Register consistently appropriate for a review in a magazine.

Organisation and cohesion
Introduction – which identifies the magazine in some way.
Clearly organised with reference to some relevant aspects.

Target reader
Would
- have a good understanding of the magazine and its contents
- understand what the writer thinks of it

Question 5 (a): The Colour of Blood

Content
Letter must describe some of the different aspects of the novel which make it compelling reading.

Answers must be supported by reference to the text. The following are possible references:
- *exciting episodes*
- *Bem's uncertainty about his enemy's identity*
- *the tense political situation*
- *interest in how Bem will deal with the situation*
- *concern for Bem's safety*

Range
Language for
- narrating
- explaining

Appropriacy of register and format
Register consistently appropriate for a magazine article.

Organisation and cohesion
Appropriate introduction and conclusion.
Clearly organised and paragraphed.

Target reader
Would
- have an insight into the theme of the novel
- understand why the writer feels the novel is a thriller 'you can't put down'

Question 5 (b): The Go-Between

Content
Essay must compare Lord Trimingham and Ted Burgess and consider their treatment of Leo.

Answers must be supported by reference to the text. The following are possible references:
- *character of Lord Trimingham*
  aristocratic, war hero
  upright and honest
  much looked up to by all at Brandham Hall
  marries Marian
- *treatment of Leo*
  is always kind to him
  takes time to talk and explain things to him
- *character of Ted Burgess*
  farmer
  reputation as 'a bit of a lad'
  shoots himself when he and Marian are discovered
- *treatment of Leo*
  treats him with deference when he knows he comes from the Hall
  is prepared to use Leo as 'postman'
  is kinder and more considerate to Leo than Marian is

Range
Language for
- describing
- narrating
- analysing
- comparing

Appropriacy of register and format
Register consistently appropriate for essay for tutor.

Organisation and cohesion
Well organised and paragraphed.
Suitable introduction and conclusion.

Target reader
Would
- learn about the two characters
- understand how the writer interprets their behaviour towards Leo

Question 5 (c): Things Fall Apart

Content
Letter must
- recommend the book
- describe the changes in Okonkwo's world
- explain how Okonkwo responds to these changes

Answers must be supported by reference to the text. The following are possible references:
- *arrival of the missionaries*
- *conversion of some important villagers*
- *new form of government*
- *new system of justice*
- *trading post*
- *sees no virtue in any change*
- *has to be stopped from killing Nwoye when he becomes a convert*
- *advises violent resistance to the white man*
- *feels nothing but unreasoning hatred for white man*
- *prepares for village meeting by wearing war dress*
- *kills leader of messengers sent to break up meeting*

Range
Language for
- narrating
- explaining
- recommending

Appropriacy of register and format
Register consistently appropriate for a letter to a newspaper.

Organisation and cohesion
Well organised and paragraphed
Early reference to reason for writing
Suitable conclusion

Target reader
Would
- understand how changes in Okonkwo's world are dealt with in the novel and his response to the changes
- be able to decide on the novel's suitability for the feature

Paper 3 Use of English (1 hour 30 minutes)

Part 1 (one mark for each correct answer)
1 with **2** despite/notwithstanding **3** doing/trying **4** What
5 not/hardly/scarcely **6** little **7** if **8** keep **9** accustomed/used
10 whose **11** a **12** given/considering/despite **13** for/with
14 most/best (NOT least) **15** the

Part 2   (one mark for each correct answer)

16 narrative   **17** successors   **18** acknowledgement   **19** authorship
20 extraordinarily   **21** popularise/popularize   **22** picturesque
23 unrivalled/unrivaled   **24** bankruptcy   **25** creditors

Part 3   (two marks for each correct answer)

26 pass   **27** mean   **28** occupied   **29** idea   **30** feature
31 gathering

Part 4   (one mark for each correct answer)

32 (a) **complete** lack/absence of trust (1) OR complete mistrust/distrust
(NOT a **complete** mistrust/distrust) + between (1)
33 made no/did not make (any/a) **reference** (1) OR did not/didn't include a/any
reference OR made not the slightest reference + to the influence (1)
34 will take place/be held indoors (1) + in the **event** of (1) OR will be an indoor
event (1) + if there is/should it/if it should/in case of/if it should (1)
35 us (all)/everyone by surprise (1) + with/by her punctual **arrival** (1)
(NOT aback / NOT **arrival** on time)
36 nothing (else) (that/which) (1) (NOT nothing more) + I'd like **more** than (1)
(NOT I'd want) OR would please me **more** than OR would give me **more**
pleasure than
37 it not been for **her** age (ALLOW **her** age been different) (NOT **her** age been
less) (1) + he would (1)
38 (got) no reason/grounds (1) + to **suppose** (that) (1)
39 (that) there is a/the **threat** (1) + of rain (for) (1) OR of it/its raining (NOT for)
(NOT that it will/may/might rain)
NB: the mark scheme for Part 4 may be expanded with other appropriate answers.

Part 5   (questions 40–43 two marks for each correct answer)

40 ruthlessly
41 granting privileges
42 that we tend to regard animals as if they were people
43 people are not interested in the fact that their ideas are wrong
44 Award up to four marks for content. The paragraph should include the
following points:
   i   their appearance is appealing
   ii they feature in children's stories – people are sentimental about them
   iii people no longer have real contact with the animal world
   iv people see some animals as symbolising certain environmental ideals

Paper 4   **Listening** (40 minutes approximately)

Part 1   (one mark for each correct answer)
1 B   **2** C   **3** C   **4** A   **5** B   **6** A   **7** B   **8** A

Part 2   (one mark for each correct answer)

9 D/dangerous T/tastes   **10** harvest(ing) (period)   **11** seed (and) berries (in either order)   **12** status symbol   **13** (for) rent(s)   **14** silk
15 ginger   **16** (burning/burned/burnt/sunburnt/sunburned) skin
17 (some/many) insects / bugs

Part 3   (one mark for each correct answer)
18 C   **19** B   **20** C   **21** B   **22** D

Part 4   (one mark for each correct answer)
23 S   **24** B   **25** B   **26** S   **27** D   **28** B

Transcript   *Cambridge Certificate of Proficiency in English Listening Test. Test 1.*

PART 1   *You'll hear four different extracts. For questions 1 to 8, choose the answer (A, B or C) which fits best according to what you hear. There are two questions for each extract.*

Extract 1   [pause]

The first science fiction film was *Rocket to the Moon*, made in 1902. According to one movie director not known for his succinct use of language, the appeal of science fiction is that 'it's the modern equivalent of ancient myths, where the fantasy world that's created provides the backdrop against which human nature can come up trumps in the face of adversity.' And ever since that first movie, we've been vicariously hurling our bodies into the void: to the moon, and above all to Mars.

For several decades Mars was a place of awe, even in, say, the 1938 film *Flash Gordon's Trip to Mars*, in which all the Martians spoke English. It seems laughably naive now.

In the 1950s, science fiction gained a tinge of science fact, not to mention politics. A decade later, the increasingly sophisticated movie-going audience was drifting away to other genres, after more convincing special effects, or out of the cinema altogether. And for a few years, there was little film-makers could do to stem the flow.

[pause]

[The recording is repeated.]

Extract 2   [pause]

Interviewer: Now Dr Peters, in your new book you talk about a superorganism, and you give the example of an ant colony, but I haven't been able to find an entry for 'superorganism' in <u>my</u> dictionary of science.

Dr Peters: Well, you see many scientists have been sceptical about the usefulness of explaining large structures in nature that seem in some way to behave like an organism, when they are not actually 'alive' in any sense that we normally use the term. Appealing, simple ideas aren't always precise, and can cause confusion.

Interviewer: So what you're saying is that the superorganism idea, of a group of organisms acting together like a larger organism, has no precise definition.

Dr Peters: Indeed. However, social insects such as ants, whose cooperation results in a whole, different and more powerful than any individual – capable of feats like keeping the temperature in the colony stable – have long been studied with interest. They are an obvious example of a superorganism.

[pause]

[The recording is repeated.]

Extract 3	[pause]

Well, I tend to make it up as I go along. I don't map out stories beforehand. You have to know what road you're going along but not what twists and turns it's going to have, but you've got to get to a destination even though you don't know what it is. But all novels are different. I've written thrillers in which you kind of have to know the plot, which I find a bit tedious actually, because then in a way you're just filling in the gaps with language. It's more stimulating if you take the reader on a route you don't know either – a magical mystery tour!

And yet you have to trust your unconscious enough to know you'll be able to tie up all the ends, and it's quite startling when you do, because you go through a patch when you're despondent. But you have to remember that this has happened before and hope it'll happen again *(laughs)* and I think I learnt early on, you know, the pain of having to abandon something is so terrible that your unconscious will do anything to avoid it, anything!

[pause]

[The recording is repeated.]

Extract 4	[pause]

Have you ever wondered why, in Western fashion, men's and women's coats and shirts do up on different sides? Is there a sensible reason for this and when did this first begin? Well, buttons were first introduced into fashion in the thirteenth century for decorative effect and started to become functional a couple of hundred years later. You don't start to see them in women's dress, however, until around the nineteenth century. The answer to the mystery seems to me to lie in the fact that upper-class women, who were at the forefront of fashion, were probably dressed by servants. Now because these servants were likely to be right-handed and would be facing the lady they were dressing, the buttons would be on the opposite side to men's, who dressed themselves. It's a kind of mirror image and the often-mooted suggestion of it having something to do with men needing to keep their sword-arms free is irrelevant, because by the time women's buttons arrived, men were no longer using swords.

[pause]

[The recording is repeated.]

[pause]

That's the end of Part One.

Now turn to Part Two.

[pause]

PART 2	*You will hear part of a radio programme in which food historian Andrew Dalford talks about pepper, one of the commonest spices. For questions 9 to 17, complete the sentences with a word or short phrase.*

You now have forty-five seconds in which to look at Part Two.

[pause]

Presenter:	Pepper is such a common food item nowadays that we have almost ceased to appreciate it. It may be hard to believe it was once so valuable it was used as currency. Food historian Andrew Dalford talks about the significance of pepper in history and in cooking.
Andrew:	Today, when spices cost so little, it seems unbelievable that these fragrant bits of bark, leaves and seeds were once so costly, so hard to track down and transport, that men were willing to risk their lives going to the ends of the earth for them. I've investigated the history of spices and written about it in *Dangerous Tastes* which has just been

published. Pepper is a unique spice, as the fruits are marketed in four different versions: black, white, green and red, according to the harvest period, irrespective of the planting and growing conditions. Yet whereas everybody knows that salt is valuable, because you need it in order to live, pepper is not essential. So why was it so sought after?

Pepper was valued partly just because it was expensive. For hundreds of years, pepper only grew in southern India, so it was a voyage of many months to bring it to other parts of the world. At the time when such journeys were hazardous, lengthy and unpleasant, the result was that the merchants could charge almost whatever price they fancied. Ships travelled from Europe with goods in huge quantities so that pepper could be brought back in exchange. Unscrupulous suppliers often mixed in commonly available berries and seeds, even small stones, to make the sacks of pepper go further. In the West it was considered exotic, yet in southern India it's a common plant – everyone can grow it in their garden, as a vine hanging off other trees.

The traffic in spices goes back to the days before recorded history. Archaeologists estimate that by fifty thousand years ago, primitive man had discovered that parts of certain aromatic plants help make food taste better. Spices have been socially important throughout history as a status symbol as well as for flavouring and preserving foods. Their value can be seen as early as the year 408, when they are featured in a list of valuable items given to Alaric the Visigoth in return for the release of the city of Rome.

Being much smaller and lighter than metal, pepper was particularly suited for use instead of money. Wealthy aristocrats kept stores of pepper as we might store gold, since everyone recognised its value as currency. It was accepted as payment for rents and debts. Pepper was considered one of the essential luxuries which were in demand in the Roman Empire along with silk and materials such as ivory, which the Romans exchanged for the pottery and leather goods they produced.

Pepper remained important down through the centuries. Spices were also used in preserving foods, as well as seasoning them to cover up the taste of food which may have been slightly rotten. Although best known, along with salt, for its flavour-enhancing qualities, pepper, like ginger, came to be used for medicinal purposes, for example, as a digestive stimulant. Its hot and pungent flavour was helpful to those with respiratory problems. When the hotness catches your throat it aids coughing, and thus the removal of offending irritants. It was also used as an external ointment to soothe itching or burning skin, especially when caused by overexposure to the sun.

Black pepper is an effective deterrent to insects as it is toxic to many of them. It can be either ground and dissolved in warm water and sprayed on plants or sprinkled on affected areas. Today, pepper, the king of spices, still accounts for one fourth of the world's spice trade. Pepper is the third most added ingredient to recipes, after water and salt. Some even like it for sweet dishes, such as strawberries. So the humble pepper has an illustrious and dramatic past which we should perhaps remember as we unthinkingly grind or sprinkle it onto our food.

Presenter: Thank you, Andrew Dalford.

[pause]

Now you'll hear Part Two again.

[The recording is repeated.]

[pause]

That's the end of Part Two.

Now turn to Part Three.

[pause]

PART 3   *You will hear part of a radio discussion about graphology, the study of handwriting. For questions 18 to 22, choose the answer (A, B, C or D) which fits best according to what you hear.*

You now have one minute in which to look at Part Three.

[pause]

Interviewer: In today's discussion we are going to examine that rather secret science, graphology – the study of handwriting. Can it really reveal our personality, strengths and weaknesses, and if so, is it a valid way of assessing the suitability of potential employees? With me in the studio, I have Richard Fielding, Chairman of the British Society of Graphology, and Maria Parker of the British Psychological Institute. Richard, can you tell us briefly what a graphologist does?

Richard: Well, a graphologist first obtains a quite lengthy sample of handwriting, such as a letter from a private client, or from a group of potential employees, and then subjects it to minute analysis, by studying the formation of the letters and the way the writing slopes to the left or the right, etcetera. You may not know that handwriting consists of three types of movement: dominant, secondary and miscellaneous. If all three types point to a certain character attribute, such as sociability or optimism, for example, or on the professional side, the ability to work well in a team, then you know that that particular attribute is genuine. Now if you don't have those different levels of proof, then you mustn't commit yourself to saying anything about that person, as far as that attribute is concerned.

Interviewer: Maria?

Maria: Well, that sounds very impressive, but, to my way of thinking, you can write down as many rules and regulations as you like for deciding what different sorts of writing are supposed to mean, but they have yet to be shown to be valid, i.e. is there really any link between the way you form your letters or your words and your personality? After all, writing is sometimes a product of education, isn't it? If you're taught to write in a certain style, that obviously influences the way you write, and how can that then be a true reflection of what you're really like?

Richard: But of course we take all of that into consideration, Maria. None of us actually writes the way we're taught at school. Not only do we not write the way we're taught, we can't. We all put our own individual slant on the basic handwriting style …

Maria: *(interrupting)* That rather proves my point, I think …

Richard: *(interrupting)* Please let me finish. I was going on to say that in graphology it's the differences between how we started out and what we're now manifesting that have everything to do with our individual pattern of psychology, and a graphologist is a person who is skilled at interpreting the symbols that appear on the page in the light of this distinction.

Maria: But surely, if you will excuse me for saying so, it's like fortune telling and horoscopes, there are elements that will apply to scores of people. The sort of interpretation you can place on handwriting is, I admit, very seductive at first sight, but I would be very wary about believing it. All the reports I've read would probably apply to a particular client and virtually everyone else on the face of the planet!

Richard: I can't go along with you there, but I do agree that there is still considerable scepticism in Britain generally. However, we are finding now that many big firms, especially those with a US connection, have adopted graphology as part of their recruitment process and find it a very successful tool, although some of them are rather loath to admit it as yet.

Maria: Isn't that rather significant?

Richard: Not really. I think it's because people like to maintain a certain sort of degree of privacy, or a low profile, about these things. It is a confidential area, after all.

Maria: As we know, various people have tried to establish whether graphology works over the years, graphologists, psychologists and others. But I think the real issue is that we don't <u>know</u> whether it works or not. It might work, I don't know, and neither does anyone else for that matter, and whilst we're not sure, I don't think it should be used for serious applications like job selection and assessment. It's fine as an after-dinner amusement or topic for a one-off class for recalcitrant teenagers on a wet Friday afternoon, but perhaps we should leave it there for the moment.

Interviewer: Well, on that note ... *(fade)*

[pause]

Now you'll hear Part Three again.

[The recording is repeated.]

[pause]

That's the end of Part Three.

Now turn to Part Four.

[pause]

PART 4 *You will hear two friends, Dominic and Sue, talking about formality in the workplace. For questions 23 to 28, decide whether the opinions are expressed by only one of the speakers, or whether the speakers agree. Write S for Sue, D for Dominic, or B for both, where they agree.*

You now have thirty seconds in which to look at Part Four.

[pause]

Dominic: You know Sue, I was speaking to someone yesterday about informality at work and he thought that open-plan offices really improve the working environment and encourage people to talk about the job and about problems among themselves, and to the boss, who's sitting there too.

Sue: I wouldn't be able to concentrate, so it would definitely be detrimental to my work output.

Dominic: Well, it depends to some extent on the individual, I suppose, but it works for me, though previously I was sceptical.

Sue: These days with e-mail and all these other ways of communicating, I can't see any advantage in having open-plan offices.

Dominic: That's hardly an argument against them. Everyone wants a more informal atmosphere these days.

Sue: Another aspect of being less formal is calling your colleagues by their first names. Where I work the owners most definitely want to be called 'Mr' and 'Mrs', but the rest of us all call each other by our first names. Does your company have any convention on that?

Dominic: We're trained to go for polite informality. I answer the phone and introduce myself as Dominic Greenfield, not Mr Greenfield, so everyone calls me Dominic and we're off on a good footing.

Sue: I'm sure that's right, because you're immediately breaking down the barrier. You can get on with the business more smoothly than if you sound starchy.

Dominic: What about dressing down at work into casual wear? My boss has changed his mind in fact, and now he thinks it's acceptable. What do you think about that?

Sue: I'm for it in the right environment. Maybe you are in a very young environment, not an old-fashioned workplace like mine and it's probably very acceptable if people, ... frankly if they work better because they feel more comfortable. But as long as it doesn't get too sloppy, because I think if you go to work with no idea of formal dress, if there isn't any code at all then it just tends to encourage people to be lazy.

Dominic:	I understand what you're saying, and maybe wearing a nice shirt and tie and a nice pair of cufflinks, … y'know, is important to impress your clients. But when you've got a day at work when you're not having any meetings or representing the firm at all, and you're probably in an airless, overheated office, I think it helps to have easy, casual clothes.
Sue:	I think modern offices are usually quite congenial and conducive to work.
Dominic:	Anyway, it shouldn't be like school.
Sue:	But I think some of the reasons children wear school uniform can be applied to adults in the workplace. I've always been in favour of school uniform because it equalises people in a place where they need to concentrate on work, not on what everybody else looks like.
Dominic:	And there are certainly those who need to be protected from their own dress sense, and it'd be better for all of us if they were told.
Sue:	What difference does that make to your performance at work?
Dominic:	Don't you think that dressing down may create an unspoken hierarchy that doesn't really exist? So people at work, who're maybe on the same level, if one of them dresses on a higher budget, in designer labels, even if it's casual clothes, that person will automatically be seen as more prestigious.
Sue:	I don't say it's all-important, but I think it could disadvantage certain people. I like the idea of being comfortable and wearing casual clothes and it all being easier and less formal, but I always feel right in a suit at work.
Dominic:	I think there's two sides to the argument.
Sue:	Anyway, I like to come home.....*(Fade)*

[pause]

Now you'll hear Part Four again.

[The recording is repeated.]

[pause]

That's the end of Part Four.

There will now be a pause of five minutes for you to copy your answers onto the separate answer sheet. Be sure to follow the numbering of all the questions.

Note: Stop/Pause the recording here and time five minutes. In the exam candidates will be reminded when there is **one** minute remaining.

[pause]

That's the end of the test. Please stop now. Your supervisor will now collect all the question papers and answer sheets.

Test 2 Key

Paper 1   **Reading** (1 hour 30 minutes)

Part 1   (one mark for each correct answer)

1 D	2 B	3 A	4 D	5 B	6 C	7 A	8 D	9 C
10 B	11 D	12 B	13 D	14 B	15 C	16 C	17 A	
18 B								

Part 2 (two marks for each correct answer)

19 C **20** A **21** C **22** B **23** A **24** B **25** C **26** D

Part 3 (two marks for each correct answer)

27 C **28** H **29** A **30** F **31** D **32** E **33** G

Part 4 (two marks for each correct answer)

34 C **35** A **36** B **37** A **38** C **39** B **40** D

Paper 2   Writing (2 hours)

Task-specific mark schemes

Question 1: Computers – our best friend or worst enemy

Content
Essay must discuss the role of computers with reference to
- access to information
- access to worldwide contacts
- computers making us anti-social and lazy – frightening consequences

Range
Language for
- attacking/defending an opinion
- presenting a reasoned argument

Appropriacy of register and format
Register consistently appropriate for essay for tutor.

Organisation and cohesion
Well-organised essay with clearly developed argument.
Appropriate introduction and clear conclusion.

Target reader
Would
- be aware of writer's assessment of the positive and negative aspects of computers
- understand writer's opinion about the role/value of computers

Question 2: Travelling on a Small Budget

Content
Report must focus on writer's region and give information about cheap
- ways to travel
- places to stay
- activities for visitors

Range
Language for
- giving information
- describing
- making recommendations

Appropriacy of register and format
Register consistently appropriate for tourist brochure.
Report format, probably with headings.

Organisation and cohesion
Clearly organised in sections.

Target reader
Would have a clear idea of what the region offers for travellers on a small budget.

Question 3: My Ideal Home

Content
The article must
- describe writer's ideal home, showing how it would reflect his/her personality
- explain what houses/furnishings reveal about people in general

Range
Language for
- describing
- hypothesising/explaining
- drawing conclusions

Appropriacy of register and format
Register consistently appropriate for article in magazine.

Organisation and cohesion
Well organised and paragraphed.
Clear introduction.
Description moving from writer's self to general conclusions about other people and their homes.

Target reader
Would
- know something about the writer's ideal home and how it reflects their personality
- understand the writer's views on what we can learn about people from the type of home they live in and the way they furnish it

Question 4: Media Coverage of Famous People

Content
Letter must
- describe media coverage in the writer's country of famous people
- evaluate the way this coverage affects their lives

Range
Language for
- describing
- narrating
- hypothesising/explaining

Appropriacy of register and format
Register consistently appropriate for letter to a magazine.

Organisation and cohesion
Clearly organised, moving from description to explanation.

Target reader
Would
- learn something about media coverage of famous people
- understand writer's opinion of the effect such coverage has

Question 5 (a): The Colour of Blood

Content
Report must
- recommend the book and include reference to the title
- provide reference to what title may suggest/significance of the title
- give analysis of what novel is about

Answers must be supported by reference to the text. The following are possible references:
- *a novel of violence*
- *description of fighting/death*
- *straightforward story of conflict*
- *complicated and exciting plot*
- *uncertainty about identity of Bem's opponents*
- *difficult political situation*
- *conflict between idealism and expediency*
- *Bem's courage and resourcefulness*
- *a wide range of different characters*

Range
Language for
- describing
- narrating
- evaluating
- recommending

Appropriacy of register and format
Register consistently appropriate for report for members of reading group.

Organisation and cohesion
Well organised and paragraphed.
Suitable introduction and conclusion.

Target reader
Would understand why the writer thinks the book is suitable.

Question 5 (b): The Go-Between

Content
Essay must
- identify the theme of the novel and explain how this is illustrated in the first sentence
- identify theme of novel
- give examples of 'differences' in the past

Answers must be supported by reference to the text. The following are possible references:
- *Leo's desire to confront the past and see the visit to Brandham Hall in its true light*
- *the unfamiliarity of life at the Hall*
- *the different social set-up Leo experienced there*
- *the way the young Leo idealised the characters*
- *the way the young Leo viewed the events, particularly the actions of Marian*

Range
Language for
- describing
- narrating
- evaluating

Appropriacy of register and format
Register consistently appropriate for essay for tutor.

Organisation and cohesion
Well organised and paragraphed.
Suitable introduction and conclusion.

Target reader
Would understand the writer's impression of the theme of the novel.

Question 5 (c): Things Fall Apart

Content
Review must examine Okonkwo's relationship with at least two of his children and say what this reveals about his character.

Answers must be supported by reference to the text. The following are possible references:
- *Nwoye*
  Okonkwo often chastises and beats him
  Okonkwo tells him stories of violence and bloodshed
  Okonkwo teaches him about farming through fear and by threats
  Okonkwo has to be restrained from killing him when he shows interest in the teaching of the missionaries
  Nwoye never returns home and is glad to leave his father
- *Obiageli*
  Okonkwo seems to have little time for her
  he does not sympathise when she breaks her water pot

> *Okonkwo gets Ezinma to explain to her about marrying someone from*
> *Umuofia*

- *Ezinma*
  Okonkwo has a special affection for her
  he wishes she were a boy
  he follows anxiously when she is carried through the forest but does not reveal
  his concern
- *Ikemefuna*
  he becomes 'like a son' to Okonkwo who does not show his affection
  Okonkwo hides how pleased he is with Ikemefuna's influence on Nwoye
  Okonkwo joins in the killing of Ikemefuna because he is afraid of being
  thought weak

Range
Language for
- describing
- narrating
- analysing

Appropriacy of register and format
Register consistently appropriate for a review for members of reading group.

Organisation and cohesion
Clearly organised and paragraphed.

Target reader
Would
- have an understanding of the relationship between Okonkwo and at least two of his children
- be able to see what this reveals about Okonkwo's character

Paper 3   Use of English (1 hour 30 minutes)

Part 1   (one mark for each correct answer)

1 what   2 bring   3 it   4 Since   5 by /through   6 any/every
7 handed/passed   8 although/though/while/whilst   9 no   10 which
11 despite/notwithstanding   12 During/Within/In/Over   13 whose
14 from   15 such

Part 2   (one mark for each correct answer)

16 dramatically   17 demanding   18 executives   19 disorientation
20 acquisition   21 outset   22 designated   23 accompany
24 sleepiness   25 enhancement

Part 3   (two marks for each correct answer)

26 running   27 cut   28 raise   29 authority   30 fresh
31 account

Part 4   (one mark for each correct answer)

32 took my sister (1) + **over** three hours to finish/do (1) (NOT I took over three hours)

33 unable / not able (1) + to find **anywhere** (1) (ALLOW to find a space / space anywhere)

34 have no **intention** / don't have / haven't got any **intention** (1) + of waiting (1)

35 fierce argument (1) (NOT fight, disagreement) + **broke** out between (1)

36 as/though I admire her (NOT like) business ability (1) + I **dislike** (1) (NOT so/than I dislike)

37 far as (1) + I am / I'm **aware** (1)

38 as the **reason** for (1) (NOT <u>a</u> reason) + the delay (1)

39 failed to / did not / didn't **live** up to (1) + the expectation(s) (1)

NB: the mark scheme for Part 4 may be expanded with other appropriate answers.

Part 5   (questions 40–43 two marks for each correct answer)

40 (the) pedigree OR family tree

41 actual or mythical ancestor (whole phrase essential)

42 Paraphrase of 'personification of history', e.g. bringing history to life through real people / understanding what the past was like through individuals/families / studying the past/history through people NOT facts/events

43 sweeping generalisations (of a few politico-economic historians)

44 Award up to four marks for content. The paragraph should include the following points:
   i   way of tracing descent
   ii bound people together in a sense of kinship/unity
   iii determining/validating royal/aristocratic succession
   iv importance of genealogies in deciding who would inherit / resolving arguments about who property/titles etc are passed onto. ALLOW could establish when surnames were first recorded.

Paper 4   Listening (40 minutes approximately)

Part 1   (one mark for each correct answer)

1 C   **2** A   **3** A   **4** C   **5** A   **6** B   **7** B   **8** C

Part 2   (one mark for each correct answer)

9 healing power(s) NOT 'powers' alone   **10** (all kinds/types of) social
11 smell   **12** tropical rainforest(s)   **13** carbon (-) dating
14 the climate / a region's climate   **15** hollow (trunks in) (trunk/trunked)
16 fuel   **17** (gradual) decay/decaying

Part 3   (one mark for each correct answer)

18 C   **19** D   **20** B   **21** C   **22** D

Part 4   (one mark for each correct answer)

23 B   **24** B   **25** S   **26** M   **27** S   **28** S

| **Transcript** | *Cambridge Certificate of Proficiency in English Listening Test. Test 2.* |

PART 1   *You'll hear four different extracts. For questions 1 to 8, choose the answer (A, B or C) which fits best according to what you hear. There are two questions for each extract.*

Extract 1   [pause]

How many of us can put our hands on our hearts and say we've never blown our top, cast caution aside and let rip in that most exquisite spasm of apoplexy, temper? Oh, we've all heard about road rage, trolley rage, you-name-it-rage; that burning frustration, threatening to explode as you wait for the shopkeeper to finish her conversation before she serves you. But despite living in a culture that positively encourages us to let it all hang out, a few of us still don't like to admit that we lose our temper. But we've all been there. Certainly as children, the stamping feet, the clenched fists, wails of fury. But as adults? Well, that's a different story. Have you ever caught sight of yourself in the mirror while in the throes of a rage? The bright red face, the huffing and puffing. When we've calmed down, we realise it's an ever-so-slightly undignified episode which most of us would like to forget and quite often do. Not that that stops us falling into the trap again.

[pause]

[The recording is repeated.]

Extract 2   [pause]

Interviewer: Michael, do you think autobiography is a less honest form than biography?

Michael: I think it's more personal, but less comprehensive. It's probably better at getting at certain aspects of the truth – childhood, relationship with parents …

Interviewer: But the problem arises, Michael, when people have an image they wish to protect, politicians, for example, rock stars and sports performers …

Michael: Well, my view is wherever facts are in dispute, trust the biography. I think public figures, their autobiographies often give themselves away inadvertently, but are not to be relied on wholly.

Interviewer: Now, you've had the experience of helping a rock star, Frank Silver, write his autobiography. What was that like?

Michael: Well, Frank has a streak of honesty, rare perhaps in his line of work. It's almost a perverse masochistic wish to be straight in the face of his image, and that in a sense is his image. When we started, Frank told me to go to Scotland and check what he remembered, with his relatives. I said, 'We don't need that, the whole point about an autobiography is, it's your view of what happened that people are interested in and it becomes a self-validating process.'

[pause]

[The recording is repeated.]

Extract 3   [pause]

What's likely to happen all over the world is that we'll see an increasing homogenisation of the earth's plant life. There's plenty of evidence to show that that's going on. I'm particularly worried about aliens; plants that have insinuated themselves into ecosystems where they don't belong. Many ecologists now believe that the spread of such aliens is the second biggest threat to the world's range of species after habitat loss.

A lot of the species we're talking about that are currently causing this problem were deliberately brought in for ornamentation but once aliens are established, it's not easy to get rid of them. They become a problem not because native ones are effete and ripe for take-over by more aggressive colonists, but because native plants have their own predators, insects, etcetera, fungal diseases. When you have an introduction into a country, it doesn't have anything that's adapted to live on it. And so the alien is able to grow very well with a release from that competition, I suppose.

[pause]

[The recording is repeated.]

Extract 4

[pause]

The next time some academic writes a book about how science is on the verge of having a grand theory of everything, he or she should be mercilessly exposed, not only for misleading us, but for encouraging us to believe that science has the answer to all our problems; that all we need to do is lie back and follow the instructions. Genetics is the most recent example of this triumphalism in science. Exaggerated news reports give the impression that a genetic cause can be assigned to virtually anything. And whilst more serious scientists make clear that that's not true if you study the evidence carefully, no-one's listening at that point because the story's broken and the headline has caught the public imagination in a way that the detail never could. The cult of the expert is a strong one. We like to believe that scientists are clever and their conclusions are valid. But we also persuade ourselves that we don't need to think things through for ourselves. Somebody else will do this for us, somebody who knows what they're talking about.

[pause]

[The recording is repeated.]

[pause]

That's the end of Part One.

Now turn to Part Two.

[pause]

PART 2

You will hear a man called Derek Lane giving a talk on the subject of ancient trees. For questions 9 to 17, complete the sentences with a word or short phrase.

You now have forty-five seconds in which to look at Part Two.

[pause]

Good evening, my name's Derek Lane and I've come to talk to you this evening on the topic of ancient trees. I've always been fascinated by such trees, given their cultural and historical significance. In the past, ancient trees were often credited with having healing powers and featured heavily in many aspects of folklore because anything that lives for thousands of years is bound to impress, providing as they do a direct link with our ancestors, with our history. Ancient trees often served as the location for important religious ceremonies as well as all kinds of social gatherings, with important local buildings being built nearby as testimony to their significance to the community.

These days, we are less impressed by such notions, but nonetheless we're becoming more aware of our ancient trees, some of which may turn out to be even older than we had imagined. For example, of those discovered so far, the creosote bush found in California is thought to live for up to eleven thousand years. The creosote bush gets its name due to its peculiar smell; it's like the tar that's used on telegraph poles to preserve the wood. It's a robust bush which grows abundantly. A research project was recently set up to discover just how many species there were worldwide which could live for over a thousand years, and at the last count had notched up seventy in all kinds of unexpected places. For example, the researchers had originally been erroneously advised to ignore places defined as tropical rainforest because life cycles in that type of environment are so rapid that ancient trees were thought to be unlikely. This led researchers to look in even more unlikely places, many of which have proved to contain old, if not ancient, specimens.

Some of this research took place in the Amazon Basin in South America. The researchers used a technique called 'carbon-dating' to find out the age of various trees and turned up trees twelve hundred, fourteen hundred years old, on a regular basis. Counting the rings in a tree trunk is now thought to be an old-fashioned way of calculating a tree's age. However, new technological developments mean that this can reveal evidence about a region's climate more accurately than if human hands had kept such records. Yet another critical reason for locating and preserving ancient trees.

One reason for the persistence of certain old trees is that they develop hollow trunks. Far from indicating that the tree is at all unhealthy, a hollow trunk provides it with greater stability in the face of strong winds, so it's a natural process of self-preservation. Not all old trees survive completely unaided of course. In Europe, one reason why so many trees have lasted so long is the system of woodland management known as coppicing. This technique, which involves cutting off the branches in a systematic way over a period of time, aims to provide a fuel source which isn't going to run out, but a useful side effect of the process is that it prolongs the life of the tree. Coppicing seems to regenerate the trees, and, barring disease or fire, some individual trees will last for thousands of years if managed properly.

Apart from marvelling at their great antiquity, there are other reasons for naturalists to prize ancient trees. Each individual tree represents a unique habitat in its own right, for it provides a complex patchwork of different microhabitats for a range of small creatures. There are something like seventeen hundred different invertebrate species in Britain alone, which are dependent on the fact that the tree trunks are in a gradual state of decay. Every one of a tree's residents has its own favourite niche and between them the various spiders, beetles, ants and flies manage to exploit every nook and cranny available.

[pause]

Now you'll hear Part Two again.

[The recording is repeated.]

[pause]

That's the end of Part Two.

Now turn to Part Three.

[pause]

PART 3

You will hear a radio discussion on the subject of dictionaries. For questions 18 to 22, choose the answer (A, B, C or D) which fits best according to what you hear.

You now have one minute in which to look at Part Three.

[pause]

Interviewer: The creation of dictionaries used to be a slow and genteel process. But these days dictionaries seem to be subject to the same pressures as any other book. I'm joined by Dr Elaine Wilson, Publishing Manager for the *New London Dictionary*, and Tony Travis, who's a professional dictionary compiler, otherwise known as a 'lexicographer'. Elaine, do you agree that competitive pressure is now there in dictionaries?

Elaine: I think it's true generally. There's an enormous market for dictionaries overseas now, for example. And I feel under a lot of pressure from management. We have to maximise the income that we make from dictionaries and of course the way to do that is to keep them as up to date as possible.

Interviewer: And how are the decisions made?

Elaine: There's a rigorous system for assessing whether a new word should go in the dictionary. We have a team of readers who go through material for us and provide us with examples. This gives us a big database. We then look at any potential new entries and what we're looking for is the frequency and breadth of use, so we want to see that a word's being used by more than one journalist, commentator, writer or speaker. And we're also looking for use in more than one level of media.

Interviewer: Tony, people say anecdotally that the influence of America is very strong because of television programmes, movies, the internet. Do we see that also in dictionaries?

Tony: Oh yes. The American domination of the media still means that a lot of the new words come from the United States. But there is a fight-back. There's a lot more Australian, Caribbean, Northern English coming into the language, mainly through slang.

Interviewer: Elaine, we talked about the internet and new technology. It must make it easier to track a word.

Elaine: Yes, it does. Much of the data-gathering that our various teams do in order to authenticate a new word or usage has been accelerated. It's also improved the compiling process because all the stages are done electronically and equipment will continue developing over the next decade or so.

Interviewer: Does it worry you, Tony, this competitive pressure?

Tony: Oh yes, and in fact I must be clear about this – this is not a totally objective profession. I mean, it's very interesting if you look at these new dictionaries, there are very few technical terms relating to farming, climbing, and fishing, for example, but there are a huge number relating to alternative medicine, the theatre and journalism. I think this says something about where the lexicographers are coming from.

Interviewer: Very briefly, both of you, doctors have this mania for finding a new disease. Do you … is it tempting to invent a word yourself to go into the dictionary? Tony?

Tony: Ah, I've been told that most lexicographers slip in at least one invention just …

Interviewer: Do you have to watch your staff on this?

Elaine: No, no, we never slip in our own invented words. That would go against everything we stand for. Anyway, we have our work cut out capturing all the genuine new words without trying to invent others! (*laughs*)

Interviewer: All right, we believe you! Elaine Wilson and Tony Travis, thank you.

[pause]

Now you'll hear Part Three again.

[The recording is repeated.]

[pause]

That's the end of Part Three.

Now turn to Part Four.

[pause]

PART 4   *You will hear part of a conversation in which two friends, Maria and Stuart, are discussing Maria's search for a new job. For questions 23 to 28, decide whether the opinions are expressed by only one of the speakers, or whether the speakers agree. Write M for Maria, S for Stuart, or B for both, where they agree.*

You now have thirty seconds in which to look at Part Four.

[pause]

Stuart: How's the great job hunt going then, Maria?

Maria: Not that brilliantly actually, Stuart. I knew it wasn't going to be easy, but I didn't realise it'd take this long.

Stuart: What kinds of posts are cropping up?

Maria: Well, there's all the usual stuff, office manager type of thing. But you know that's what I was doing in my last job and I just got fed up with it. You see, I sort of feel I want a job with some sort of ethical dimension. I've had enough of all this corporate business somehow.

Stuart:	Big companies do seem horrifically greedy, don't they?
Maria:	They're just interested in making a profit. I feel I want to put something back in, if you know what I mean. So I was thinking about working for a charity.
Stuart:	Hmm, interesting. But they must be short of funds. You don't want to end up working for peanuts in some dingy little back office somewhere with a broken-down old typewriter!
Maria:	Well, I wouldn't put up with that. Anyway, I think most charities seem to be pretty professional organisations these days.
Stuart:	I can't see myself working anywhere except the smart end of town and having a state-of-the-art computer. And a photocopier that works!
Maria:	The thing I'm most worried about is getting stuck with one organisation. Who knows, I might change my mind about all this and move on to something completely different, and then something else, and so on. In fact, the more I think about it, the more likely that seems.
Stuart:	Well, I'm not going to be in shipping forever, you know. I think we're all bound to be moving into other fields sometime in our lives. I'm certainly thinking along those lines. I just wonder though, Maria, if you'd be able to move up the ladder in a charity as easily as in a big firm. You've got to think of your career.
Maria:	I don't suppose it's much different from any other organisation. If you get on well with colleagues and managers, you stand a pretty good chance of making progress.
Stuart:	Mind you, I got made Marketing Manager last month and the boss and I have never really hit it off.
Maria:	You'll have to put that right! By the way, Stuart, did you sign a contract when you started work for Transatlantic?
Stuart:	I didn't actually. I don't know why, must have been an oversight.
Maria:	Doesn't sound much like you. Shouldn't you look into it? Might find you're suddenly out of a job.
Stuart:	I'll worry about that when it happens. *(pause)* You know, I almost envy you in a way. It must be quite fun, knowing there are all these opportunities out there. Somewhere there's the perfect job for you!
Maria:	Suppose nobody wants me! That's more nerve-racking than anything else.
Stuart:	But it'd be great to have a job you were really proud of. It says something about you, don't you think, the work you do?
Maria:	I'm not too bothered about how people see me, really. What I'm concerned with is my own feeling about it, that's all.
Stuart:	Well, I can't wait to see what … *(fade)*

[pause]

Now you'll hear Part Four again.

[The recording is repeated.]

[pause]

That's the end of Part Four.

There will now be a pause of five minutes for you to copy your answers onto the separate answer sheet. Be sure to follow the numbering of all the questions.

Note: Stop/Pause the recording here and time five minutes. In the exam candidates will be reminded when there is **one** minute remaining.

[pause]

That's the end of the test. Please stop now. Your supervisor will now collect all the question papers and answer sheets.

Test 3 Key

Paper 1   Reading (1 hour 30 minutes)

Part 1   (one mark for each correct answer)

1 B	2 D	3 A	4 C	5 D	6 A	7 D	8 B	9 D
10 B	11 A	12 C	13 C	14 D	15 C	16 A	17 B	
18 C								

Part 2   (two marks for each correct answer)

19 A	20 B	21 D	22 A	23 D	24 C	25 B	26 C

Part 3   (two marks for each correct answer)

27 F	28 C	29 H	30 G	31 D	32 A	33 E

Part 4   (two marks for each correct answer)

34 B	35 A	36 D	37 C	38 A	39 C	40 B

Paper 2   Writing (2 hours)

Task-specific mark schemes

Question 1: Attitudes to Work

Content
Letter must discuss attitudes to work with reference to
* pay
* working hours / holidays
* job satisfaction

Range
Language for
* explaining
* presenting and developing an argument
* comparing and contrasting ideas

Appropriacy of register and format
Register consistently appropriate for a letter to the editor of a radio programme.

Organisation and cohesion
Early reference to reason for writing.
Clear organisation of ideas.
Suitable conclusion.

Target reader
Would understand the writer's own views about work.

Question 2: Film Review

Content
Review must
- identify and describe the film with reference to the writer's country
- assess the film's effectiveness in illustrating life and attitudes of that country

Range
Language for
- describing
- narrating
- explaining
- evaluating

Appropriacy of register and format
Register consistently appropriate for a review.

Organisation and cohesion
Clear introduction.
Well-organised description/narration leading to evaluation.
Appropriate conclusion.

Target reader
Would know
- what the film is about
- how well the film portrays some aspects of life and attitudes in the (writer's) country

Question 3: New Shopping Centre

Content
Report must give information about new shopping centre and refer to
- design and atmosphere
- transport provision
- influence on people's shopping habits

Range
Language for
- describing
- explaining
- evaluating

Appropriacy of register and format
Register consistently appropriate for a report written for one's manager.

Organisation and cohesion
Introduction.
Well-organised report, possibly with headings.
Appropriate conclusion.

Target reader
Would
- have clear information about the shopping centre – design, atmosphere and transport
- have some ideas of the effect the centre seems to be having on shopping habits

Question 4: Significant Inventions

Content
Article must
- describe at least one invention or discovery
- explain its significance to the development of civilisation

Range
Language for
- describing
- explaining
- evaluating

Appropriacy of register and format
Register consistently appropriate for an article in an English language newspaper.

Organisation and cohesion
Appropriate introduction.
Clearly organised ideas.
Suitable conclusion.

Target reader
Would
- have a clear picture of the invention/discovery
- understand why the writer thinks it is/they are so significant

Question 5 (a): Things Fall Apart

Content
Letter must
- explain that the ideas like justice, love and duty will mean the novel appeals to a worldwide audience
- refer to specific episodes to illustrate the writer's point of view

Answers must be supported by reference to the text. The following are possible references:
- *justice*
  importance of respecting law – the death of Ikemefuna
  banishment of Okonkwo
- *love*
  Okonkwo's affection for his daughter Ezinma
  Ikemefuna's growing affection for his new family
- *duty*
  importance of observing tribal customs and festivals (e.g. week of peace)
  Okonkwo's sense of doing what is 'right' leads to his suicide

Range

Language for
- describing
- narrating
- explaining
- analysing

Appropriacy of register and format
Register consistently appropriate for a letter to a magazine.

Organisation and cohesion
Reference to reason for writing.
Clearly organised ideas.
Suitable conclusion.

Target reader
Would
- understand why the themes described in the novel will appeal to a worldwide audience
- have some idea of how these are illustrated in the novel

Question 5 (b): Bel Canto

Content
Essay must
- describe how imprisonment affects the lives of two of the hostages
- consider to what extent imprisonment gives them a sense of freedom

Answers must be supported by reference to the text. The following are possible references:
- *for all hostages, imprisonment*
  releases them from worry, concern for the future
  exposes them to a great deal of music
  gives freedom to express feelings that normally remain hidden
- *Gen meets and falls in love with the girl from the jungle*
- *Mr Hosokawa can form relationship with Roxanne*
- *Roxanne – her singing seems to put her in charge of the life in the house*
- *Ruben Iglesias takes pleasure in 'ordinary' pursuits – cooking, gardening*
- *Father Aguedas is able to help people, and is appreciated for what he does*
  Fyodorov is emboldened to express his feelings

Range

Language for
- describing
- narrating
- explaining
- comparing and contrasting

Appropriacy of register and format
Register consistently appropriate for an essay for tutor.

Organisation and cohesion
Clearly organised ideas.
Suitable introduction and conclusion.

Target reader
Would know
- something about two of the hostages
- to what extent they gained a sense of freedom

Question 5 (c): An Inspector Calls

Content
Article must
- outline Mr Birling's views on society
- consider Eric and Sheila's response to the evening's events with reference to their family background

Answers must be supported by reference to the text. The following are possible references:
- *he says a man has to mind his own business and look after himself and his own*
- *as a businessman he believes in keeping down costs at the expense of workers*
- *he is happy to accept prestige but not responsibilities of his position*
- *his major concern – avoid public scandal, keep up appearances*
- *Eric has rebelled and scandalised his parents*
- *the revelations help him to analyse and judge his parents' attitudes*
- *Sheila's behaviour in shop – to be expected from her upbringing*
- *revelations make her sympathetic towards Eva Smith and she develops a sense of guilt*

Range
Language for
- describing
- narrating
- analysing

Appropriacy of register and format
Register consistently appropriate for a magazine article.

Organisation and cohesion
Clearly organised ideas.
Suitable introduction and conclusion.

Target reader
Would understand
- Mr Birling's views on society
- the influence their upbringing had on Eric and Sheila, as illustrated by their response to the evening's events

Paper 3   Use of English (1 hour 30 minutes)

Part 1   (one mark for each correct answer)

1 above   **2** each   **3** same   **4** as   **5** have (ALLOW get/keep/see)
6 most   **7** between   **8** take   **9** way   **10** which   **11** well
12 ourselves   **13** possible (NOT ever, before)   **14** result/consequence
15 about

Part 2 (one mark for each correct answer)

16 substantial (ALLOW substantive)   **17** underestimated (ALLOW underestimated)   **18** enabled   **19** emphasis   **20** adherence
21 anatomical   **22** suspicion   **23** noticeably   **24** seductive
25 significance

Part 3 (two marks for each correct answer)

26 break   **27** settle   **28** fired   **29** allow   **30** tear/pull
31 handle

Part 4 (one mark for each correct answer)

32 change(s) of/in policy / policy change / policy changes (1) + **took** everyone/
everybody by (1)

33 after (many) years of saving / saving for years / having saved for years (NOT
with many or finally) / many years' saving **did** (1) + Celia (finally) manage
(NOT she) (1)

34 **speed** at/with which (1) + the rumour spread (NOT was spread) (1) OR **speed**
of (1) + the rumour's spreading (1) (ALLOW **speed** which/that the rumour
spread with) OR **speed** ... with (1) + which the rumour spread (1)

35 kept/left his/the staff (1) + (completely/totally) in the **dark** (1)

36 from **being** embarrassed (1) + by her daughter's (NOT his) (1)

37 is **reputed** to be (1) + a reliable and dedicated (1)

38 (can) get (1) + **hold** of (1)

39 in (ALLOW with) the **hope** (1) (NOT because they had a hope) + of making
(it into) / getting into / being selected for (1) OR (that) they would/might make/
get into

NB: the mark scheme for Part 4 may be expanded with other appropriate answers.

Part 5 (questions 40–43 two marks for each correct answer)

40 (to) barricade (yourself against) NO OTHER ADDITIONS.

41 (the/a) (slightest) lack of concentration/commitment/focus/willpower/drive to
work.
Link with 'work' essential. ALLOW easily distracted from work (not just
'easily distracted'). Paraphrase of 'motivation' essential BUT ALLOW answers
which change the form of motivation e.g. not very motivated to work and
ALLOW answers which use 'motivation' but then go on to explain it e.g. lack
motivation and, therefore, don't have the ability to concentrate on work.
Penalise incorrect interpretation of 'slightest' e.g. NOT a complete/big lack of

42 (our) basic instinct. NO OTHER ADDITIONS.
43 (the/a) soul-destroying prison. NO OTHER ADDITIONS.
44 Award up to four marks for content. The paragraph should include the following points:
    i Provides essential separation between home and workplace.
      ALLOW keeping work and home separated is beneficial.
      Separation between home and work necessary for health.
      Enables worker to concentrate on work.
      There are fewer distractions at work.
    ii Work creates a feeling of self esteem / boosts the confidence of people at work.
      Gives people the status of working.
      Gives the satisfaction of having a real job.
    iii Work offers a ready-made social network / circle of friends.
      Work provides individuals with the chance to feel part of a team / something bigger than themselves (which is a basic human need).
    iv Sometimes work gives people an escape from an unsatisfactory private/ personal life.
      Work helps people to forget about problems at home. NOT just domestic chores.

Paper 4   Listening (40 minutes approximately)

Part 1   (one mark for each correct answer)
1 B   **2** C   **3** C   **4** A   **5** A   **6** B   **7** A   **8** B

Part 2   (one mark for each correct answer)
9 barn   **10** round/circular   **11** brick(s)   **12** wooden
13 (the) water pipes/pipes for the water/plumbing   **14** waterproof
15 extractor fans   **16** row of houses   **17** urban areas

Part 3   (one mark for each correct answer)
18 B   **19** C   **20** D   **21** D   **22** B

Part 4   (one mark for each correct answer)
23 S   **24** J   **25** B   **26** B   **27** S   **28** J

Transcript   *Cambridge Certificate of Proficiency in English Listening Test. Test 3.*

PART 1   *You'll hear four different extracts. For questions 1 to 8, choose the answer (A, B or C) which fits best according to what you hear. There are two questions for each extract.*

Extract 1   [pause]

    Two spacecraft were launched in 1977. On each is a Golden Disc containing information such that, should it ever fall into the tentacles of advanced space-faring civilisations, they'll know something about us and the little rock we live on. On it can be found readings in many human languages, and also music. It seemed appropriate to say something about who we are, what our feelings and aspirations are, and this is conveyed by no more satisfactory means than music. Is it possible that the soaring emotions which so many of the pieces represent will be entirely a mystery to them? Would they find it totally incomprehensible, strangely beautiful, immediately understandable?

What other life forms make of these strange noises is anybody's guess, but in the meantime the spacecraft are heading outwards carrying out their number-one function of sending back data about the nature of the space between the stars. The clock is ticking and their power source will not last forever. But even when their instruments are dead, they will continue to take our humanity into remote space for eternity in the hope that we're not alone.

[pause]

[The recording is repeated.]

Extract 2   [pause]

At the outset, I should point out two things about my recent research paper on the subject. Firstly, you will often find philosophical ideas applied to, or tested by, the concrete experience of individuals. For this I make no apology; an idea has to bear the weight of concrete experience or else it becomes a mere abstraction.

Secondly, I've disguised individual identities rather more heavily than one would when reporting formal interviews; this has meant changing places and times and occasionally compounding several voices into one or splitting one voice into many. These disguises put demands on the reader's trust, but I am not, in any case, looking for the type of trust a novelist would seek to earn through a well-made narrative, that sort of coherence is lacking in real lives. My hope is that I have accurately reflected the sense of what I've heard, if not precisely its circumstances.

[pause]

[The recording is repeated.]

Extract 3   [pause]

Lucy: New technology must have offered enormous potential over the last decade in your work as a TV journalist, hasn't it?

John: We've got user-friendly video tape now, so you simply put in a cassette and film whatever you want. You come back, put it into another machine and edit.

Lucy: So that means you must rush things just to get something out on air without having considered its true worth.

John: That issue comes up way before that; when you decide what to shoot and what to ignore. If you're lucky, you have the luxury of choice, but there are thin days with very little action.

Lucy: But how do you know how what you film will fit into the news context of any given day?

John: You don't when you're out there on the street. You just have to go with your gut reactions. And it's surprising how much good news doesn't appeal to the eye.

Lucy: The result must be disjointed in the context of the whole news programme that we the public later see.

John: That's the skill and experience of the editor; not to let you see the joins or perhaps I should say the cracks!

[pause]

[The recording is repeated.]

Extract 4   [pause]

One of the things I'm trying to do here is actually to unwrite my own writing, re-imagine the writing, destroy it, rough it up. When we began editing the film, we assembled it in story and scene order, and that ran at about 4 hours 35 minutes, which is a bit long for even the most generous audience. So obviously our aim is to try and bring the film down to a pleasurable length without damaging it. It's rather like when you're remodelling or renovating a house. Necessarily, in order to make sense of the film, we've had to smash through walls, we've had to rearrange the original architecture, and that makes an enormous mess. So what were sometimes quite elegant transitions, where the grammar of the film was perfectly easy to follow, all that's been destroyed by this process of 'how can we shorten this film sensibly?' It's interesting work, but in the process there's dust everywhere, there are cracks, there's a lot of residual destructive elements to be tidied up. We're still reducing the film, but now we can plan the decorating.

[pause]

[The recording is repeated.]

[pause]

That's the end of Part One.

Now turn to Part Two.

[pause]

PART 2   *You will hear a woman called Gill Firth talking about how she builds houses and other buildings out of straw. For questions 9 to 17, complete the sentences with a word or short phrase.*

You now have forty-five seconds in which to look at Part Two.

[pause]

Good evening. I've come here to talk to you about the buildings I design and build, using what some people view as a somewhat unlikely material: straw. Now as you know, straw is the dried stalks of grain plants, like wheat and barley, long used for making things like baskets and hats, and, in many parts of the world as a traditional roofing material. And it makes good walls too. Although what you see is a solid wall, it's actually constructed out of blocks made of compressed straw which are then plastered and painted.

I've only been building in the material for five years, but interest is certainly on the increase. I've completed sixteen projects in that time, everything from retirement bungalows on the coast of Scotland to stable blocks in central London, and my latest project is an extension which I'm building onto a barn at a Scottish farm. The owner is converting it into a bed and breakfast hostel, for walkers in particular because this area attracts a lot of visitors. It's a fairly exposed spot, so I've gone for a round construction, which will be more stable in the heavy winds that are common here than, say, a rectangular one would be.

I use bales of straw which are largish compact blocks, manufactured in regular sizes, which you place one on top of another in a set pattern. It's not unlike laying bricks. A wider range of skills is needed because although the construction is wholly straw-based, other materials are used to hold the blocks in place. The first row of straw bales I secure into the foundations using metal pins, but after that all the pinning is done with wooden pins. I prefer them because it's a much more sustainable material and it works just as well.

Then, when the wall is in place, it's covered with plaster on both the outside and inside, so what you see is a normal wall, there's no straw showing anywhere. We've put all the water pipes and the electrical wiring in behind the plaster as we build, so it's very nearly ready for use. Now the thing that surprises most people about this project is the fact that this extension is actually going to be used as a shower room, and you're all probably thinking the same thing, 'But won't it affect the straw?' Well, surprisingly, this is not a problem. Indeed with these walls it's not necessary for us to waterproof, because straw breathes naturally, unlike concrete, and wetness is not usually a problem. Of course, bearing in mind the eventual use of the structure, we are also fitting extractor fans. That's called for under government regulations whatever material you build in.

So, if a building like this works in this kind of location, you can see what the possibilities are for building in straw in the future. What I'm trying to do now is get together the investment to build a whole row of houses in this material. This is a much larger project, as you can imagine. But I do think it's the way forward, because the materials are not expensive and the technology is not too complicated, so it's something that communities could do for themselves, especially in urban areas. It's quite possible to build lovely two-storey, high-density dwellings at a fraction of the cost of the faceless mass-produced construction projects that are now the norm.

There's been lots of interest in straw buildings from all over Europe … *(fade)*

[pause]

Now you'll hear Part Two again.

[The recording is repeated.]

[pause]

That's the end of Part Two.

Now turn to Part Three.

[pause]

PART 3   *You will hear an interview with a woman called Alice Cowper, who went in search of a rare animal called the king cheetah. For questions 18 to 22, choose the answer (A, B, C or D) which fits best according to what you hear.*

You now have one minute in which to look at Part Three.

[pause]

Interviewer: The story of the king cheetah, until recently thought only to be a legend, fired the imagination of Alice Cowper. She told me how she and her husband, Peter, set out on a journey to prove that the king cheetah really does exist.

Interviewer: What actually does it look like? How does it differ from a normal cheetah?

Alice: It is an absolutely magnificent-looking cat, and for people who know anything about spotted cats, the cheetah is the obvious spotted cat. It's always spotted, but this animal, instead of having spots, it's got thick, broad, black stripes, about the thickness of a man's thumb, three to five running down its spine from the ruff of the neck right down to the base of the tail. And the rest of it is just covered in blotches, like ink blots, which are a marvellous fingerprint. But, apart from that, the fur is fractionally longer, fractionally silkier than the normal cheetah.

Interviewer: So, you established that it did exist. You established the area of Africa where you might find it and then you actually went out into the bush to look for it?

Alice: That's right.

Interviewer: How did you go about it?

Alice: Well, we had to prove that the animal was existing now and it was simply a matter of elimination. In Botswana, we came up with no hard evidence, no animals that we could photograph or film, but after about fourteen months, we got film and photographs in a National Park of all places. In fact, they didn't know that they had a king cheetah there, it was the only one at the time, since then the number has increased.

Interviewer: So you're not saying this is a new species?

Alice: No, it's actually a mutation and mutations are simply nature trying out a new pattern, a new style. Normally, they're just colour pattern changes, and they're generally one-offs, they just crop up now and again.

Interviewer:	It's the consistency of this mutation that interests you, though, isn't it? You don't regard it as just another mutation, do you?
Alice:	That's right. Over sixty specimens is a lot. You then look at that pattern and why it's there. It's camouflage. It suits scrubland and woodland, which is not what you associate with cheetahs normally, and more of them are appearing in the wild. I think it's clear that what we are seeing is an environmental adaptation actually taking place before our eyes.
Interviewer:	What is it about the colour pattern of the king cheetah that gives it an advantage in woodland?
Alice:	Cheetahs have enemies. Now, the king cheetah pattern is a perfect example of, perhaps the best ever, of what we call disruptive camouflage. It breaks up the shape of the animal so that it's harder to decipher it, to actually focus on what it is, and by the time you've worked out what it is amongst the trees, it's gone. So what you're looking at in the king cheetah, in that pattern, is a successful mutation. And it is working well in the environment into which the animal is moving, so much so that you're getting more of them, not less.
Interviewer:	So, we're right at the beginning of this new branch of the cheetah family.
Alice:	That's right and it's fantastic, isn't it? It's particularly exciting for people, for their sense of wonder, for their belief in the fact that it's not the end of the road, it's just the beginning. You talk to the average person and they really think everything is dying out. I had someone say to me recently, 'The real adventurers these days are the camera people', and I thought, 'Oh dear, have we come to that?' and I said, 'No, you're wrong, there's still so much to do when it comes to the wildlife out there, there are so many exciting areas that we can still follow up on, that it's not the end, it's actually just the beginning'. If you've got something adapting to new conditions, now, a big mammal, that's not depressing, that's fantastic, it says that we haven't destroyed anything.

[pause]

Now you'll hear Part Three again.

[The recording is repeated.]

[pause]

That's the end of Part Three.

Now turn to Part Four.

[pause]

PART 4	*You will hear part of a radio programme in which two people, Jim and Sue, are discussing physical exercise. For questions 23 to 28, decide whether the opinions are expressed by only one of the speakers, or whether the speakers agree. Write J for Jim, S for Sue, or B for both, where they agree.*
	You now have thirty seconds in which to look at Part Four.
	[pause]
Jim:	Have you seen the latest statistics about the high percentage of people in Britain and the United States who are failing to take enough exercise, presumably because of their increasingly sedentary lifestyles, being office-bound during the day, stuck behind the wheel of the car and then lounging on the sofa in front of the telly in the evening? Worrying, isn't it?
Sue:	Yes, I saw that report, Jim. But I also read some figures about the amazing way gyms and exercise clubs are springing up across the country, which surely suggests that we must be getting fitter as a nation. That's rather encouraging, isn't it?
Jim:	Yeah, well it certainly <u>would</u> be if it were true. I'm inclined to think these centres are springing up, as you say, to cash in on mankind's gullibility.

Sue: Are you saying that people fall for all the latest pronouncements by the TV gurus on diet, exercise, vitamin and herbal supplements, etcetera?

Jim: No, that's not what I meant, although that's certainly true for a large section of the population. No, I was thinking about the way most people realise deep down that taking more exercise would be beneficial and so they make the effort to join a gym or start an exercise programme, with every intention of making it a part of their lives. But it's just too hard, the workload or demands from family and friends intervene and after a few weeks they're right back to square one.

Sue: Not everyone gives up, Jim, but I take the point that there's a lot to squeeze into the average day, especially as more and more people commute long distances to work. I wonder if motivation has a part to play here?

Jim: In the way that people have to seriously want to get fit or it won't work?

Sue: That undoubtedly helps, of course, I was thinking more about group motivation. If you're going to run by yourself every morning, it's all too easy to talk yourself out of it if it's drizzling or you're feeling a bit below par, while if there are a number of friends running together or going to the gym at set times, you have peer group support to keep you going and give you a pat on the back when you've achieved something.

Jim: Hmm, and looking at the other side of the coin, it's less easy to bow out because you have to face the disapproval of other members of the group.

Sue: We've been talking about exercise as something which is done in the increasing leisure time we're supposed to be enjoying now, so it has to involve an element of choice. What about exercise as part of the daily work routine?

Jim: Do you mean jobs which involve a lot of physical labour such as farming, or are you thinking of employers insisting that their workforce does an exercise session once or twice a day?

Sue: I was thinking more of the latter. It's a way of breaking up the day, toning you up and preventing some of the problems which can occur when sitting too long in one position, as well as the drowsiness of course.

Jim: I'm sure there are obvious advantages for the bosses in terms of increased work output … maybe I'm just too much of an individualist. I couldn't endure the idea of enforced physical activity, it sounds too much like school to me. On the other hand, companies making sports facilities – gyms, pools, etcetera – available to their staff in their lunch hour or before and after work seems less authoritarian and therefore more appealing.

Sue: Aren't we back to the old problem of still having to make a personal commitment to using the facilities and then trying to stick to it?

Jim: It's a vicious circle, you mean? I suppose that's so, a bit like a running track, then?

Sue: Very apt! *(laugh)* … *(fade)*.

[pause]

Now you'll hear Part Four again.

[The recording is repeated.]

[pause]

That's the end of Part Four.

There will now be a pause of five minutes for you to copy your answers onto the separate answer sheet. Be sure to follow the numbering of all the questions.

Note: Stop/Pause the recording here and time five minutes. In the exam candidates will be reminded when there is **one** minute remaining.

[pause]

That's the end of the test. Please stop now. Your supervisor will now collect all the question papers and answer sheets.

Test 4 Key

Paper 1　Reading (1 hour 30 minutes)

Part 1　(one mark for each correct answer)
1 B　　2 A　　3 C　　4 A　　5 B　　6 D　　7 A　　8 C　　9 B
10 C　　11 B　　12 D　　13 C　　14 A　　15 A　　16 B　　17 C
18 D

Part 2　(two marks for each correct answer)
19 D　　20 B　　21 A　　22 C　　23 D　　24 B　　25 A　　26 D

Part 3　(two marks for each correct answer)
27 D　　28 F　　29 H　　30 B　　31 G　　32 A　　33 C

Part 4　(two marks for each correct answer)
34 C　　35 B　　36 A　　37 C　　38 A　　39 D　　40 B

Paper 2　Writing (2 hours)

Task-specific mark schemes

Question 1: Letter

Content
Letter must discuss position of young people today with reference to
- labour-saving devices
- increased opportunities
- increase/decrease in happiness as a result

Range
Language for
- describing
- narrating
- presenting and developing an argument

Appropriacy of register and format
Register consistently appropriate for a letter to a newspaper.

Organisation and cohesion
Clear reference to reason for writing.
Well-developed argument.
Discussion leading to a conclusion.

Target reader

Would

- understand the writer's views on the life and opportunities for young people
- know whether the writer thought young people are happier now than people were in the past

Question 2: Physical Qualities and Success in Sports

Content

Article must consider

- physical qualities necessary to become a successful sportsman/woman
- whether mental qualities can result from participating in sport

Range

Language for

- describing
- narrating
- explaining

Appropriacy of register and format

Register consistently appropriate for a magazine article.

Organisation and cohesion

Clearly organised ideas.

Suitable introduction and conclusion.

Target reader

Would understand the writer's views on

- physical qualities needed by successful sportsmen and women
- mental qualities which may be developed by sportsmen and women

Question 3: Radio Programme for Young People

Content

Proposal must put forward suggestions for a successful programme for young people with regard to

- content
- structure
- style of presentation

Range

Language for

- giving information
- explaining
- recommending

Appropriacy of register and format

Register consistently appropriate for a proposal submitted to a radio station.

Organisation and cohesion

Clearly organised proposal, probably with headings.

Suitable introduction and conclusion.

Target reader
Would have a clear idea about the programme, as proposed by the writer, in terms of content, structure and style.

Question 4: Comedy in the Cinema

Content
Letter must
- identify and describe a film
- give reasons for including it in the festival

Range
Language for
- describing
- narrating
- recommending
- explaining

Appropriacy of register and format
Register consistently appropriate for a letter to the organiser of a film festival.

Organisation and cohesion
Early explanation for reason for writing.
Clearly organised ideas.
Appropriate conclusion.

Target reader
Would know
- why the film made the writer laugh
- why it was being recommended

Question 5 (a): Things Fall Apart

Content
Essay must
- describe the impact of the changes on Okonkwo's life
- assess the role the changes played in Okonkwo's death

Answers must be supported by reference to the text. The following are possible references:
- *loss of son Nwoye to the missionaries*
- *Okonkwo's return to Umuofia is disappointing because of the changes*
- *many people won over by establishment of trading store*
- *imprisonment over burning of the church*
- *he realises, after he kills the messenger, there will be no war. This lack of support leads him to suicide*

Range
Language for
- describing
- narrating
- explaining
- analysing

Appropriacy of register and format
Register consistently appropriate for an essay for a tutor.

Organisation and cohesion
Suitable introduction and conclusion.
Well-organised ideas.

Target reader
Would
- understand the impact of the changes on Okonkwo's life
- realise how far these changes contributed to his death

Question 5 (b): Bel Canto

Content
Article must
- describe the relationship between Gen and Carmen
- show how danger influences the development of the relationship

Answers must be supported by reference to the text. The following are possible references:
- *Carmen must obey the Generals*
- *conflict of divided loyalty for Carmen*
- *they risk detection by other hostages*
- *secret meetings at night*
- *limited opportunities to speak to each other*

Range
Language for
- describing
- narrating
- explaining

Appropriacy of register and format
Register consistently appropriate for a magazine article.

Organisation and cohesion
Suitable introduction and conclusion.
Well-organised ideas.

Target reader
Would
- understand the relationship between Gen and Carmen
- know how the dangers surrounding them influenced the development of their relationship

Question 5 (c): An Inspector Calls

Content
Letter must
- explain what makes it different from other detective stories
- refer to the nature of the 'crime' that's being investigated in the play

Answers must be supported by reference to the text. The following are possible references:

- *usually a single guilty person is revealed by proof that eliminates suspects*
- *in this case, everyone is guilty or implicated*
- *detectives usually deal with motive/opportunity*
- *this inspector knows everything from the beginning*
- *it is the 'suspects' who learn what they have done*
- *the 'crimes' involved are greed, hypocrisy, selfishness, self-interest, lack of concern for others*

Range
Language for
- describing
- narrating
- explaining

Appropriacy of register and format
Register consistently appropriate for a college magazine article.

Organisation and cohesion
Explanation of reason for writing.
Clearly organised ideas.
Suitable conclusion.

Target reader
Would understand
- what makes the play unusual as a detective story
- the nature of the 'crimes' involved

Paper 3   Use of English (1 hour 30 minutes)

Part 1   (one mark for each correct answer)

1 its   **2** everything/anything   **3** too   **4** where/wherein   **5** like
6 fail   **7** comes   **8** worth   **9** were/was   **10** one   **11** According
12 for   **13** below/beneath   **14** which   **15** being

Part 2 (one mark for each correct answer)

16 incomprehensible   **17** psychologists   **18** countless   **19** originate
20 unexpectedly   **21** enigmatic/enigmatical   **22** unknown
23 mysteriously   **24** independently   **25** happenings

Part 3 (two marks for each correct answer)

26 word   **27** missed   **28** taste   **29** good   **30** short   **31** kept

Part 4 (one mark for each correct answer)

32 is **rumoured** (NOT was / has been) (1) + to have accepted/taken/got (NOT found) (1)

33 (real) expectation/hope (NOT expectations) (1) + **of** the plan / plan's being/ becoming (1)

34 the **exception** (1) + of marketing (NOT the marketing) (1)

35 is (really) keen **on** (doing) (1) (NOT thrives on) (ALLOW enjoys spending time on) + is (1)

36 **bears** no / not the least/slightest (1) + resemblance/similarity to (NOT likeness/relation) (1) (ALLOW inclusion of appropriate intensifiers, e.g. whatsoever / at all)

37 (main) **reason** for going to / having gone to / visiting / having visited London (1) + <u>was</u> (1)

38 **are** (going) to be (NOT supposed/expected) (1) + consulted about/over/on/ regarding/concerning (their) (1)

39 no (way of) **escaping** (ALLOW from) (1) + the fact <u>that</u> (1)

NB: the mark scheme for Part 4 may be expanded with other appropriate answers.

Part 5 (questions 40–43 two marks for each correct answer)

40 People moving about on foot (ALLOW 'pedestrians') get in the way of / hold up traffic. / Pedestrians / non-drivers are a nuisance. Paraphrase of '<u>obstacle</u>' essential.

41 (the) device

42 absurd ALLOW addiction

43 People can be persuaded to share cars. Car-sharing can be made to work. Idea of change in attitude must be present. (Penalise answers that merely describe the car-sharing scheme).

44 Award up to four marks for content. The paragraph should include the following points:

   i Cities are built in such a way that people have to use their cars / planning decisions have promoted reliance on cars / people must travel long distances for work/shopping/school.

   ii Feeling of power it gives the driver.

   iii People want to be independent.
     Value the flexibility the car offers.
     Control their environment

   iv People can avoid the discomfort of <u>public transport</u> / walking in polluted streets.

Paper 4   Listening (40 minutes approximately)

Part 1   (one mark for each correct answer)

1 A   2 B   3 C   4 B   5 C   6 A   7 C   8 A

Part 2   (one mark for each correct answer)

9 (upside-down / upturned) dishes (upside-down / upturned)

10 enemies/predators   11 (the) winter (time)   12 (the) wind(s) (on the sea) NOT wind effects NOT wind movement   13 sandy beaches / beaches of sand

14 human(')s head / person(')s head / man(')s/woman(')s head NOT 'head' alone

15 (quite) shallow   16 heart(-)rate, heart(-)beat(s) NOT movement

17 internal organs NOT 'organs' alone

Part 3 (one mark for each correct answer)

18 D **19** C **20** A **21** B **22** B

Part 4 (one mark for each correct answer)

23 T **24** B **25** T **26** B **27** B **28** H

Transcript	*Cambridge Certificate of Proficiency in English Listening Test. Test 4.*

PART 1

You'll hear four different extracts. For questions 1 to 8, choose the answer (A, B or C) which fits best according to what you hear. There are two questions for each extract.

Extract 1 [pause]

We were living in Zambia and my parents took me to the Victoria Falls. I must have realised even then that every fall has its own character. Big is not always beautiful. A lacy ribbon spilling over a cliff can change mood and appearance on the whim of the sun going behind a cloud. Likewise, with a roaring cascade, even the note can differ. Falls are as capricious as they are complex, visually and audibly. You can visit the same fall three days in a row and find that one day it's aloof, the next it's having a tantrum with such fury that one backs away. And the day after, it will be gurgling with affection. Falls come and go, so only the big year-round ones are marked on maps. Many dry up in summer and spring into life only after rain. That's why I use contours on the map to assess where a fall might be. Then, when I want to take a photograph, I calculate the angle of light at dawn to achieve the maximum effect. Then I sit and wait for a passing shower.

[pause]

[The recording is repeated.]

Extract 2 [pause]

Interviewer:	So, Professor, what do restorers do?
Professor:	Restorers work on old paintings which are anything from one century to seven centuries old and are, as a result, covered with layers of discoloured varnish and grime. The main aim of restoration is to give people a sense of being able to look at the works without the veil of ages. Restorers can release a painting, not back to its pristine state which is sadly not feasible, but to something which gives some feeling of the real liveliness the painting had when it was first painted.
Interviewer:	Some critics say we should leave the paintings alone, as by stripping off the old varnish and cleaning them we're creating a lot of disharmonies and getting further away from what the artists intended.
Professor:	Well, in my view, responsible restorers are in effect making a choice based upon both science and aesthetics as to how a painting can look best in terms of the demands we make on the paintings. There is in a sense a period choice to be made, but every period has made that choice and choosing not to intervene is a kind of period choice as well.

[pause]

[The recording is repeated.]

Extract 3 [pause]

First there was a production line, and then a factory, and then a vacuum cleaner like no other in the world, in silver with yellow trim, working on new principles. All a tribute to John's belief that the product is *right*. Two million have now been bought and it's the biggest-selling cleaner in Britain, outstripping the established manufacturers. The Dixon empire is now centred on a massive factory in the south of England, full of new machinery and cool colours chosen by John's wife.

With a thousand people already employed by the firm, it's now in the middle of a huge expansion. A purpose-built plant next door is due to open next summer, meaning the output will double. In a world of high technology, many business people now find manufacturing much less inspiring than services or manipulating data. But John is passionate about the thing – something which distinguishes him from most of the people in British business.

[pause]

[The recording is repeated.]

Extract 4

[pause]

We inhale it, eat it and walk around in clouds of it. But in spite of the size and ubiquity of its tiny particles, dust is far from unimportant; can even have world-shaping impact. Take the soils of Jamaica and Barbados: they began life as sand, blown a speck at a time from the Sahara Desert.

In *The Secret Life of Dust*, Hannah Holmes dates her obsession with dust to a visit to the Gobi Desert. This slim volume represents an enthrallingly non-technical glimpse into this unexpectedly fascinating field of study and Holmes' enthusiasm shines through, along with her admiration for the people who investigate it. Dust researchers have to be meticulous and imaginative as they try to capture the tiny specks of evidence they spend their lives analysing. Holmes interviews dozens of them, and her thumbnail sketches give a vivid impression of fellow obsessives tramping across deserts and up volcanoes to collect samples, and then teasing the secrets from their miniscule catches.

[pause]

[The recording is repeated.]

[pause]

That's the end of Part One.

Now turn to Part Two.

[pause]

PART 2

You will hear part of a lecture on the subject of jellyfish. For questions 9 to 17, complete the sentences with a word or short phrase.

You now have forty-five seconds in which to look at Part Two.

[pause]

What could be nicer on a hot summer's day than a cooling swim from a sheltered beach? But sometimes our swimming companions are best given a wide berth; many a holiday dip has been ruined by an unwelcome brush with the tentacles of a floating jellyfish. So, how to identify them? A jellyfish looks something like a couple of upside-down dishes and if you imagine that the central part of the lower dish has been removed, there's a mouth in that position. Around the rim there may be many long fine tentacles which extend and which in many species are used for stinging.

Jellyfish don't have many enemies – very few things eat them, basically because they are 97% water – it's like eating a soggy lettuce leaf really. They also have a gelatinous texture and, of course, they have a sting. But, for all that, jellyfish seldom live long; in fact, many of them only live for one year, so during the winter time they die off. Some small ones that will develop into the big jellyfish lie attached to rocks and overhangs in sheltered positions and then later they'll grow to full size, they'll reproduce and that'll be their lifecycle.

Jellyfish have a tendency to swarm – that is, they don't all consciously decide to swarm, in fact they have very limited control over where they swim. They're very vulnerable to wind effects on the sea and to tidal movements. Sometimes jellyfish and human beings come together and the consequences can be rather painful. This is because jellyfish get carried into sheltered bays, by the same processes which create sandy beaches.

There are many different kinds of jellyfish, and the one most commonly encountered, in Britain at least, is the box jellyfish. This has a body size up to roughly that of a person's head, and sixty tentacles trailing behind it, giving an overall length of around three metres. It floats along near the coast with these tentacles strung out in an attempt to catch its main prey, which is all sorts of small fish and crustaceans. They're inclined to turn up in swarms in quite shallow areas where they can be quite tricky to see, especially if the water is sunlit too. So when people rush into the water unawares, they can run into what seems like a curtain of tentacles. It's not very nice and then it's difficult to avoid getting stung.

So, what should you do if this happens? Now, when jellyfish sting, your initial reaction is to start running away, get out of the water as quickly as possible. But, actually, the more you run, the faster your heart rate becomes, and the quicker the venom is absorbed. So, actually, the first thing to do is to calm down the person who's been stung. It's also been shown that you can neutralise any tentacles that are still on the person's body by the application of vinegar.

But not all jellyfish sting. For example, the blue-coloured moon jellyfish is common around Britain. It won't harm you and it's a beautiful sight. You can see its internal organs because it's virtually transparent and these seem to glow in the dark in this lovely blue colour. So they're well worth looking out for.

Other varieties which you might spot include … *(fade)*

[pause]

Now you'll hear Part Two again.

[The recording is repeated.]

[pause]

That's the end of Part Two.

Now turn to Part Three.

[pause]

PART 3

You will hear part of an interview with Hal Jordan who has recently written a book on the history of music. For questions 18 to 22, choose the answer (A, B, C or D) which fits best according to what you hear.

You now have one minute in which to look at Part Three.

[pause]

Presenter: In the studio we have Hal Jordan, eminent classical composer and music historian. Hal has written a fascinating book, tracing the major breakthroughs in the history of music. Now I'd like to start at the wrong end, so to speak, *(laughs)* and ask you, Hal, what effect you think computers have had on music and composing in particular?

Hal: Well, the most obvious one is practical. A composer can use a computer like a word processor to speed up the whole business of writing the parts for individual instruments in an orchestral piece. But like the innovation of word processing for writers, umm, it has to some extent changed the psychology of the way we write as well, because you can try things out that you wouldn't have tried before. So I think that's one thing, although there's a catch to all this which is that only someone who can *read* music can tell whether what the computer has come up with is right. And what we spend all our time doing is correcting what the computer has produced, but I'm not sure what's going to happen in fifty years' time when people no longer know what music's supposed to look like.

Presenter: But computers take some of the drudgery out of your work.

Hal: Certainly, but some composers have also used them to play games with music, you know, by introducing the chance principle, where you just let the computer choose notes. What's interesting is that, in this experiment, we're bypassing the human ear, which has always been crucial in assessing music. And after a while, everybody's realised it's a blind alley.

Presenter: But not a complete waste of time, surely? Culturally, things happen for a time until something becomes a convention and then it's absolutely necessary creatively to break that convention. Perhaps machines can help us do that.

Hal: Absolutely. Machines generally have had a huge effect on music and the most obvious one is the invention of recorded sound at the end of the nineteenth century. Unpredictable things ensued, for example – um – that music from one culture was carried to another, mixed with it and started a third form of music. Or the fact that audiences started to hear music they were unaccustomed to and this affected how they listened, the way they heard their own music.

Presenter: Looking at earlier breakthroughs, how was music passed on before people worked out a system for writing music down on paper – notation I believe it's called, isn't it?

Hal: Correct, yes. Well, it was done largely by memory or by someone singing it to someone else, as simple as that. Oddly enough, the invention of notation in Europe in about the year 1000 was the first big step that took Western music away from other forms of music, because elsewhere people never really cracked it. They kept to the traditional way, which involved memory and improvisation, so music happened spontaneously. What notation did was that it said 'This is what it's like today and we can perform it tomorrow exactly the same. We can hand it to someone who's never met us, if they're suitably proficient, and they'll play it as well'.

Presenter: Except they don't, do they?

Hal: Not exactly, but it's closer than any other system's ever been. And the other thing was it gave you a graphic layout for music and it meant you could have architecture for music, you could build structures you couldn't possibly conceive of just by improvising, or singing to your mate.

Presenter: So, it shifted the balance of power from the performer to the composer?

Hal: Before that, all performers were composers in a way, because they were making it up as they went along. Still in some Eastern music, and European folk music too, the composer and the performer are the same person.

Presenter: This reminds me of the impact of writing on language. Some linguists talk about the invention of writing having cost us dear, as it removed us from the spontaneity of process and fixed it more in place.

Hal: Except that it's also true that the spontaneous version of music carried on alongside, notation was just another tool. Take jazz which is an African-Western amalgamation in which people improvise and yet it's intermingled with the techniques of notation. Some listeners believe erroneously that jazz is chaotic, while the musicians are actually working to a prearranged pattern, like a map if you like, but instead of having it set out in front of them, it's in their heads.

Presenter: And so, let's turn to … *(fade)*

[pause]

Now you'll hear Part Three again.

[The recording is repeated.]

[pause]

That's the end of Part Three.

Now turn to Part Four.

[pause]

PART 4   *You will hear two colleagues, Tina and Harry, talking about the problems of traffic congestion in their city. For questions 23 to 28, decide whether the opinions are expressed by only one of the speakers, or whether the speakers agree. Write T for Tina, H for Harry, or B for both, where they agree.*

You now have thirty seconds in which to look at Part Four.

[pause]

Harry: Hi, Tina. You look a bit frazzled. What's up?

Tina: Oh, Harry, you wouldn't believe the traffic! It's even worse than ever this morning. I put it down to the fact that they've brought those new bus lanes into use.

Harry: Well, the fact that the buses now have priority over cars on some roads is meant to solve the traffic problem, not make it worse. I came by bus as usual and I got here at my normal time.

Tina: There you are, that just goes to show. If the system was working properly, then you'd be getting here in half the time; as it is you're no better off and I've been held up to no avail.

Harry: It's a nice idea Tina, but actually there is no bus lane on my route, they said that the road wasn't wide enough, remember, unless they cut down all those trees and there was a public outcry. Anyway, who says it's to no avail. If it means you'll consider taking the bus in future, then maybe it's achieved its objective.

Tina: Umm … I hadn't thought of it in that way. That would be absolutely typical of our city council, wouldn't it? Anyway, that may work for some people, but to tell you the truth, I just don't fancy sitting on a bus and that's all there is to it.

Harry: Yes, and that's how a lot of people feel unfortunately, and I have to say I find it rather a selfish attitude Tina. This city's traffic problem is not going to improve unless we all work at it together, and that means everybody making certain sacrifices, like using their cars less. I don't think people mind that, actually.

Tina: OK, don't get on your high horse. I guess we've all got used to a certain degree of personal freedom, and the car plays a pretty large part in that. No-one's going to give that up willingly, you know.

Harry: I suppose the scheme does represent an attempt to restrict people's freedom, but I welcome that, if you ask me, it's not before time. And let's face it, if the road's gridlocked and you can't get to work, you've lost your personal freedom in any case.

Tina: That may be the case, but at least no-one's telling me how I should lead my life. It's alright for you, the bus takes you virtually door-to-door and you live right next to that supermarket. What about when I want to go out after work or get my shopping on the way home? It's quite a long walk from my flat to the bus stop, you know, and they aren't as frequent on my route either.

Harry: OK, I take your point, but look at it this way. If most people habitually took the bus, and only fell back on their cars when they had some bona fide reason, like your trip to the supermarket, that would still be a great improvement on everyone leaping into the car without giving it a moment's thought, whenever they wanted to go somewhere. It's the unnecessary trips that cause all the hold-ups actually.

Tina: Now I don't doubt for a moment that you're capable of doing that Harry, but I scarcely know anyone else who's in a position to even try. What about all the people with kids who've got to do the school run and still get to the office on time?

Harry: Well the kids can get the bus like everyone else.

Tina: No, that'll never happen, Harry. Mind you … *(fade)*

[pause]

Now you'll hear Part Four again.

[The recording is repeated.]

[pause]

That's the end of Part Four.

There will now be a pause of five minutes for you to copy your answers onto the separate answer sheet. Be sure to follow the numbering of all the questions.

Note: Stop/Pause the recording here and time five minutes. In the exam candidates will be reminded when there is **one** minute remaining.

[pause]

That's the end of the test. Please stop now. Your supervisor will now collect all the question papers and answer sheets.

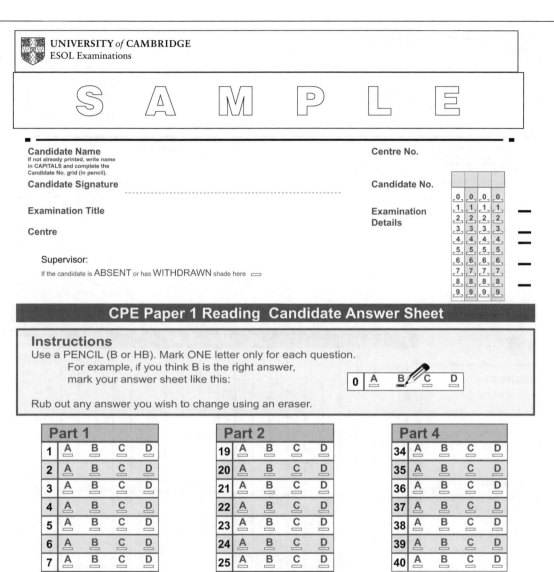

Sample answer sheet: Paper 3

S A M P L E

Candidate Name
If not already printed, write name
in CAPITALS and complete the
Candidate No. grid (in pencil).

Candidate Signature

Examination Title

Centre

Supervisor:
If the candidate is ABSENT or has WITHDRAWN shade here

Centre No.

Candidate No.

**Examination
Details**

0	0	0	0
1	1	1	1
2	2	2	2
3	3	3	3
4	4	4	4
5	5	5	5
6	6	6	6
7	7	7	7
8	8	8	8
9	9	9	9

CPE Paper 3 Use of English Candidate Answer Sheet 1

Part 1

Do not write
below here

Instructions

Use a PENCIL
(B or HB).

Rub out any answer
you wish to change
using an eraser.

For **Parts 1, 2** and **3**:
Write your answer
clearly in CAPITAL
LETTERS.
Write one letter in each
box.

For example:

| 0 | M | A | Y | | |

Answer **Parts 4 and 5**
on Answer Sheet 2.

Write your answer
neatly in the spaces
provided.

You do not have to
write in capital letters for
Parts 4 and 5.

1   1 1 0

2   1 2 0

3   1 3 0

4   1 4 0

5   1 5 0

6   1 6 0

7   1 7 0

8   1 8 0

9   1 9 0

10   1 10 0

11   1 11 0

12   1 12 0

13   1 13 0

14   1 14 0

15   1 15 0

188

Part 2

		Do not write below here
16		1 16 0
17		1 17 0
18		1 18 0
19		1 19 0
20		1 20 0
21		1 21 0
22		1 22 0
23		1 23 0
24		1 24 0
25		1 25 0

Part 3

		Do not write below here
26		1 26 0
27		1 27 0
28		1 28 0
29		1 29 0
30		1 30 0
31		1 31 0

Continue with Parts 4 and 5 on Answer Sheet 2 ▶

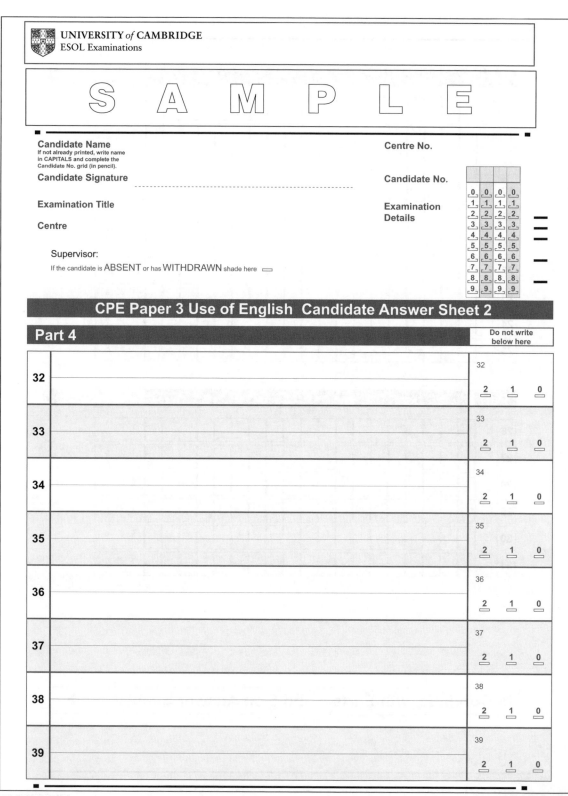

Part 5

		Do not write below here
40		40 1 0
41		41 1 0
42		42 1 0
43		43 1 0

Part 5: question 44

For Examiner use only

Marks

Examiner number: Team and Position

Content	0	1	2	3	4

Language	0	1.1	1.2	2.1	2.2	3.1	3.2	4.1	4.2	5.1	5.2

```
0  0  0  0
1  1  1  1
2  2  2  2
3  3  3  3
4  4  4  4
5  5  5  5
6  6  6  6
7  7  7  7
8  8  8  8
9  9  9  9
```

Sample answer sheet: Paper 4

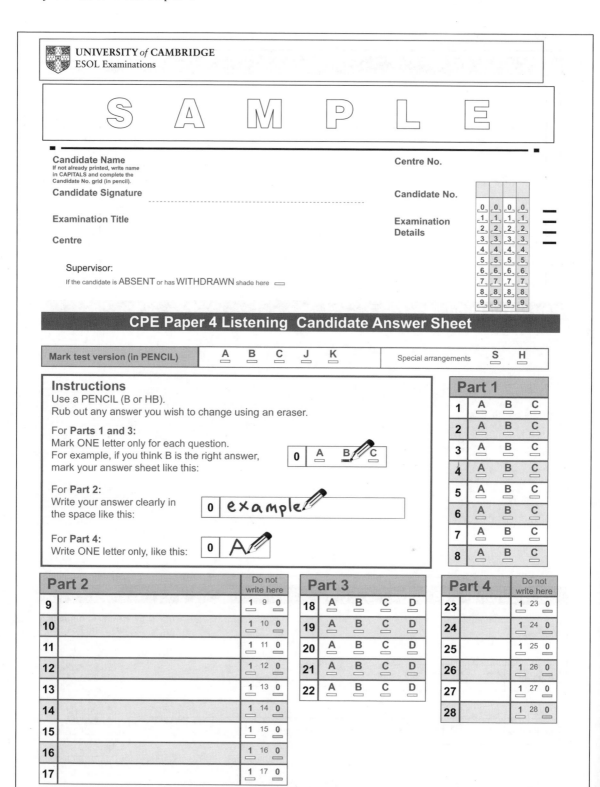